The Ultimate
Freelancer's
Guidebook

The Ultimate
Freelancer's
Guidebook

LEARN HOW TO:

Land the Best Jobs

Build Your Brand

Be Your Own Boss

Yuwanda Black

adamsmedia
Avon, Massachusetts

Published by
Adams Media, a division of F+W Media, Inc.
57 Littlefield Street, Avon, MA 02322. U.S.A.
www.adamsmedia.com

ISBN 10: 1-4405-9678-6
ISBN 13: 978-1-4405-9678-0
eISBN 10: 1-4405-9679-4
eISBN 13: 978-1-4405-9679-7

Printed in the United States of America.

10 9 8 7 6 5 4 3 2 1

Library of Congress Cataloging-in-Publication Data

Black, Yuwanda, author.
The ultimate freelancer's guidebook / Yuwanda Black.
Avon, Massachusetts: Adams Media, [2016]
Includes bibliographical references and index.
LCCN 2016014815 (print) | LCCN 2016023886 (ebook) | ISBN 9781440596780 (pb) |
ISBN 1440596786 (pb) | ISBN 9781440596797 (ebook) | ISBN 1440596794 (ebook)
LCSH: Self-employed. | Vocational guidance. | BISAC: BUSINESS & ECONOMICS /
Careers / General. | BUSINESS & ECONOMICS / Careers / Job Hunting. | BUSINESS
& ECONOMICS / Project Management.
LCC HD8036 .B53 2016 (print) | LCC HD8036 (ebook) | DDC 658--dc23
LC record available at https://lccn.loc.gov/2016014815

Cover design by Frank Rivera.

This book is available at quantity discounts for bulk purchases.
For information, please call 1-800-289-0963.

For my mother, Geraldine, who instilled in me a sense of fearlessness, the importance of education, and self-confidence. I love, honor, and miss you every day.

❋

Contents

Acknowledgments

To my friends and family: thanks for your patience as I cut you short on phone calls, left messages unacknowledged for days (sometimes weeks), and declined invitations so I could adhere to deadlines.

To my sister, Cassandra, in particular for telling me, "You can do it; just a little longer," when I was dead tired and didn't see a way to finishing.

To Acquisitions Editor Eileen Mullan (Adams Media), for approaching—and entrusting—me to write this book. Thank you for this opportunity. It was a career milestone I'll forever cherish. You were a joy to work with.

To Developmental Editor Peter Archer (Adams Media), for making this book so much better than it would have been with his insightful edits. Thank goodness for your keen eye!

Introduction

More Americans are going freelance every day—some by choice; some forced by circumstance. No matter how you may arrive at this career option, with the right information, you can thrive as a freelancer. It doesn't have to be a scary, challenging road. It can be rewarding, exciting, and fulfilling— with a step-by-step guide to help you chart your path to success. And that's what this guide is. You'll learn everything from how to write a business plan, to how to market for clients, to how to brand your freelance business.

The twenty-first-century's global economy has laid the foundation for the demand of a freelance workforce. For those willing to seize the opportunities presented, the sky is literally the limit.

Here's to your success!

Chapter 1

The Freelancer Mindset

Independent Contractor.
　Contract Worker.
　Freelancer.
　No matter what you call them, these types of workers are becoming increasingly common. In many companies across the country using freelancing services is becoming the new norm.
　Millions are taking the leap into this career path, once considered a nontraditional career option. Consider the following stats. Although they vary according to source, one thing they all make clear is that freelancing is here to stay.

- Eighty percent of large corporations say they plan to "substantially increase" their use of a flexible workforce, shifting from hiring full-time employees to using "free agent" employees.
- According to "Freelancing in America," a survey conducted by Upwork and the Freelancers Union, a staggering 53 million U.S. workers, 34 percent of the workforce, are now freelancing.

　What is it about freelancing that's attracting these enormous numbers of people? After all, freelancing can be scary, since it doesn't offer the security of a regular job with health benefits and a steady paycheck.

In fact, freelancing is a great alternative to a traditional job. But you have to get in the right mindset. Once you do that, the advantages can be enormous.

Why Freelance? Why Now?

Stop and ask yourself the question. Don't answer vaguely with something like, "I hate my job!" That may be true, but making a decision based on a negative emotion is usually much less productive than deciding because of a positive one. Instead of "I hate my job," how about, "I want to follow my passion."

For example, if your passion is paragliding, think, "How can I monetize this?" Are there paragliding classes in your area? If not, as a freelancer can you offer such classes? If there are already classes, how many outlets offer them? Could your geographic area support one more teacher offering classes? Just because there's competition does not mean that your idea is not a good one; it just means you have to do some investigating.

Practically no idea under the sun is new. That means that no matter what kind of freelance business you start, you are going to have to prepare a business plan to see if it's feasible.

The bottom line: figure out why you want to freelance because that's what will motivate you to push through any angst, fears, and stumbling blocks you may encounter along the way.

Some other benefits of freelancing include the following.

Job Security

With just over a third of the American workforce engaged in some form of freelancing, an argument could be made that freelancing is the new job security.

"But," you may be thinking, "as a freelancer, I'll only be as successful as my next gig. And the more people who are freelancing, the more competition I'm facing, which doesn't lead to job security."

Excellent point.

However, consider this: As a full-time employee, you're only as secure as your current employer says you are, because all your financial eggs are in one basket. If the parent company in Europe decides the U.S.-based branch in Dallas isn't as profitable as it should be, your company could be sold, reorganized, or go out of business. Where does that leave you? Potentially without a job.

When you freelance, you rely on more than one client/customer. If one of them disappears (is sold, reorganized, or goes out of business), they don't take your whole paycheck with them because your financial eggs are always in several baskets.

Up-to-Date Skill Set

Freelancing forces you to keep your skills sharp. Because you have to be constantly in tune with what competitors in your niche are doing, you have to consistently upgrade existing skills and acquire new ones.

Two valuable skills that freelancing hones to perfection are marketing and customer service. If you're not consistently marketing to get new clients in the door and providing excellent customer service to existing clients, you'll soon find yourself without any clients.

In short, freelancing motivates you to keep your soft and hard skill sets sharp. It's vital to staying competitive.

Work with Your Body Clock

Do you fight the urge to throw your alarm clock across the room each morning? Do you feel the most energized from 5 P.M. until midnight? Is morning your least favorite time of day? As a freelancer, you can work with your natural body clock, instead of fitting it into a predetermined schedule made up by someone else.

"But what about deadlines?" you say. "You have to make your deadlines. You can't just work when you want." Yes, you do have deadlines, but when you freelance, starting at the contract stage you determine what those deadlines are. As long as you are disciplined enough to meet them, whether you work from 5 P.M. to 9 A.M. or 9 A.M. to 5 P.M. is up to you. Think of it this way: freelancing is not a *pass* to work "when you want"; it's a *gift* to work "at your best."

Vacation

Do you have vacation time circled on the calendar in your cubicle, typed to pop up on your cell phone, and saved as a favorite on your laptop? Do you worship the word like it's a second coming of a deity you didn't even know you worshipped? How nice would it be to make it just a word again, instead of two weeks of a whole year you live for as if your very life depended on it.

As a freelancer, your vacation is not something approved by someone else. Finished up a project? Got paid? Noticed a special to Miami on Expedia for four days and three nights of fun in the sun?

Go! It's your prerogative—no need to request time off, hope your boss approves, and/or worry about if you have enough vacation days left.

Take Control of Your Financial Future

As a freelancer, you set your income goals. You don't have to wait for an annual bonus or raise, which usually isn't enough to cover the cost of inflation.

Set Life Priorities

Miss putting your kids on the bus and being there to meet them when they get off? Wish you could visit your aging aunt Matilda in the nursing home more often? Want to volunteer for the upcoming community garden project?

Freelancing allows you the flexibility to fit life around your priorities, to meet the needs of children, parents, and other people, places, things, and causes that are important to you.

Play to Your Strengths

Freelancing capitalizes on your strengths, whether they're artistic, technical, mathematical, intellectual, or something else. When you build a business that plays to your strengths, you're much more likely to enjoy the work, which underscores the final benefit.

Happiness

A 2015 study by Upwork (formerly Elance-oDesk) in conjunction with the Freelancers Union reported that 60 percent of freelancers started freelancing by choice, and half of them said that they wouldn't stop freelancing for any amount of money.

Freelancing makes many professionals happy.

Whatever your reason for wanting to become a freelancer, motivation is the key. Working for yourself is challenging not because the tasks are too difficult or complicated but because you're the only person you have to answer to if you don't get out of bed every morning and get to work.

Eight Habits of Successful Freelancers

If you freelance, it says something about who you are; the same as if you were a doctor, actor, or rodeo cowboy. The very nature of this career choice suggests that it attracts those who are different. However different freelancers may be, though, there are some traits they tend to share.

1. They Are Self-Motivated

It's easy to stay fired up when you first decide to do something. It's an adrenaline rush—this new, shiny goal that's going to change your life and turn you into the person you always wanted to be. Who wouldn't be excited by that? But then, reality sets in. You have to fit your ambition into a thing called . . . life. Things get in the way.

Successful freelancers are different. They stay motivated to achieve their goals, in spite of life's challenges. They're determined to succeed, no matter the odds.

If you're not a naturally self-motivated person, don't worry, it's something you can change. Put a routine in place. It can be as simple as meditating for five minutes every morning or creating a vision board, to something as involved as hiring a success coach. Here are five ways to get motivated:

- *Focus on the end goal.* Determine what you want. What's the end goal? What will happen once your goal is accomplished? Will you be able to finally put a down payment on a house? Make that last payment on your student loans? Have a year's worth of emergency funds in the bank? Whatever it is, focus on that.
- *Reward yourself.* Always dreamed of taking a boat trip down the Nile? Want that chocolate-colored leather bomber that's always been just a bit too extravagant for your budget? Dreaming of a scoop of double-fudge ice cream that's never on the diet list? Rewards . . . they're not just for kids!
- *Set time limit.* Putting a time limit on your perceived "torture" helps you to get started. Usually, getting started is the hard part. Once you start, you wind up putting in much more time.
- *Develop a "fighting mantra."* It's your call to battle when you realize that you're procrastinating or don't feel motivated. It can be as unoriginal as "I deserve success!" or "Get up and get moving now!" Whatever gets you off your tokus, make that your mantra.
- *Create a to-do list.* Write down a few things you want to accomplish within a defined time. Don't list too many things, or it can scare you. There's something about crossing things off a to-do list that's very motivating, so get busy and get that pencil ready to strike through completed tasks.

Motivation, like any other habit, is something that can be learned. Figure out what works for you, then practice doing it on a consistent basis. After a while, you'll find that you need "tricks" less often because being motivated will become a part of how you operate as a freelancer.

2. They Know When to Take Action

Have you ever met someone who is always talking about doing something but can't nail down a start date to save his life? Many wannabe self-employed people fall into the "research" trap. They take class after class after class, read blog after blog, consult expert after expert—but they never actually start. Mark Cuban of *Shark Tank* fame calls them "wantrepreneurs."

Successful freelancers are well aware that it is impossible to know everything before you start freelancing. In fact, there are some things you can only find out after you start. But the beauty of starting is, it's never as bad as you think. Also, thanks to the Internet and the networks of contacts you'll build, there will practically always be a source you can tap to shed some light on whatever problem you're facing.

By all means, do your due diligence on whatever niche you're targeting with your services. But ultimately you've got to take the first step and get started. It's the only way down the yellow brick road of successful freelancing.

3. They Are Risk Takers

Understandably, striking out on your own as a freelancer scares the bejesus out of you—especially if you are ensconced in a cushy nine-to-five job. Why would you expose yourself to the risks associated with freelancing: lack of insurance, uncertainty about your income, and so on?

But risk doesn't have to be a bad thing. In fact, a keen awareness of risk and a willingness to undertake it is actually a good thing when you freelance. Why? Because freelancing forces you to assess the pros and cons of various situations. It forces you to think in-depth about your career and the path it's taking.

Deciding to freelance is one of the biggest risks you'll ever take. Once you make the leap though, you'll know how to mitigate that risk by following the same strategies any other successful business owner uses: know your numbers, get pricing right, target the right market, and so on.

Now . . . does that sound risky, or smart?

4. They Figure Things Out

In the business world, people who discover solutions are called problem solvers. But when you freelance, not everything is exactly a problem. It's just something that you have to figure out.

For example, let's say you start a marketing business, helping businesses to brand themselves online. You land a new client. She forwards you tons of data to go through to learn more about her business and the direction she wants to take it.

There's only one problem. The data is in an Excel spreadsheet. You were expecting Word files and maybe a few PDF files, not spreadsheet after spreadsheet. Furthermore, the new marketing manager sends a note. She wants you to parse the data and your recommended findings in Excel and get them back to her within a week.

You've never worked in Excel in your life! Eek! The deadline has been set, the contract signed, and the deposit is sitting snugly in your account. There's only one thing you have to do: figure out how to work in Excel.

Period.

Freelancing presents a wide range of challenges, and the number and kind always increases—especially as you grow your business. So you must be good at figuring stuff out—many times, quickly.

5. They Are Disciplined

As a freelancer you decide everything from what needs to be done, to when and how, to how much to charge, to whom to hire and fire. Clients depend on you to deliver when you say you will. You'll do whatever it takes to accomplish that.

Most importantly though, you are accountable to yourself—to the dream you decided to build. It takes a strong internal drive and honed self-discipline to stay true to this.

For example, imagine you sign a contract on March 11 to complete a job by March 23. There's only one fly in the ointment—your parents' thirtieth anniversary is on March 20—and you're in the middle of planning for more than 100 family members who are flying in from across the country.

You could have turned down the contract, but it's for a client you've been trying to rope in for the past six months. Turning them down was not an option, and you know that if you knock this project out of the park, repeat work from this one company alone could be worth its weight in gold from an industry reputation standpoint. So what do you do? You immediately prioritize what needs to get done, when, by whom, and how.

- Does this mean hiring a party planner to assist?
- Does it mean outsourcing part of the project?
- Does it mean putting off your marathon training runs for the next four days?
- Does it mean getting up three hours earlier each morning?

Whatever it is, you do it because there are two things you are sure of: your parents will have the celebration they deserve; and you will finish the job on time because your reputation is on the line.

6. They Are Organized

Organization is tremendously important to freelancers—after all, if you're not organized, there's no one else who's going to do it for you. If you can't find that file the client sent detailing the changes he wanted, or you're lax checking your e-mail and you miss an important message, if you miss a project due date because you thought it was Wednesday and it was Tuesday, you'll lose clients and ruin your reputation.

Successful freelancers figure out quickly that they must get and stay organized. Not only will it allow you to handle your work flow more efficiently, it will position you to take advantage of opportunities that may come your way.

Many people do not start out super organized. However, if you recognize you've got a problem in this area, you must take steps to correct it.

An Extra Day in Your Workweek?

Research on time management published in the *Harvard Business Review* revealed that workers were able to free up nearly a fifth of their time—an average of one full day a week—just by eliminating and/or delegating unimportant tasks, and replacing them with value-added ones.

This is what time-blocking does. It keeps you on track by forcing you to eliminate distractions, do away with procrastination, and avoid unproductive multitasking.

TIME-BLOCKING TIPS

- *Determine long-range plans.* You should always have a big-picture assessment of your business in mind.
- *Decide on weekly goals.* What makes for a week well spent? Write out a few (three or four) tasks that you'd like to complete for that week. Make sure these are getting you closer to your big-picture goals.
- *Break down workday into hours.* If you work eight hours a day, assign hours to specific tasks. This way, you can see at a glance what you're supposed to be working on.

In Chapter 8, we'll talk about some productivity and organizational tools to help get—and stay—organized.

7. They Are Reliable

It's critically important to your freelance success to do what you say you're going to do when you say you're going to do it. This is really the key to building a strong client list. People learn that they can rely on you to meet deadlines and produce material in a competent, professional manner.

Make it a habit to overdeliver when possible—on time, every time. *Never, ever miss a deadline.* This one golden rule can land you more business over time than you can imagine. Your clients know that if they give you a project, there's never a doubt of you not coming through.

8. They Are Good Communicators

Many freelancers work alone most of the time. However, the most successful freelancers never lose their communication skills—which means both effective communication and listening. Without face-to-face communication, a lot can get lost in translation. Good freelancers don't rely exclusively on e-mail but instead use a range of communication devices: phone, Skype, social media, and so on.

You must be clear and exact so that there's no chance of being misunderstood, which can cost you—and your client—in time and money.

> **FREELANCER TIP**
>
> Make note of how many of these traits you already possess, and how many you need to work on. Don't despair if you don't have some of them. All of them can be developed. Just be honest with yourself as you go through the list—and start working on those areas where you feel you fall short.

If you're confident you have these eight traits—or that you can easily acquire them—it's time to take the next step and mentally prepare for the freelance life.

How to Mentally Prepare to Freelance

One of the most difficult things for many aspiring freelancers is the uncertainty that comes with this career choice. It can be downright scary wondering if you're going to earn enough to keep a roof over your head and pay your bills, keep up your healthcare, student loan payments, and so on.

You'd be crazy not to be scared.

This is why mental preparation is so vital. Following are four things you can do to get mentally fit to freelance.

Prepare for Pushback

One of the things that may surprise you when you announce that you're going to start freelancing is the resistance you'll get from friends and family. You may be well prepared to handle the "Are you crazy?" arguments from acquaintances and coworkers, but when pushback comes from those close to you, it can cause you to doubt yourself—and abandon your freelance business dreams altogether.

How can you counter this sort of thing? Most important, have a very clear idea of what you expect from your freelancing career and why you're doing it. Create healthy boundaries to prevent others from impeding your success; if they truly have your best interests at heart, they'll accept that this is your career choice.

Embrace Rejection

Rejection is just fear—fear of being told, "No. Go away. We don't need or want you or your services. You're nowhere near qualified enough to work with us. Don't ever, ever contact us again. Leave us alone!"

Of course, this is hyperbole, but when you're rejected, it can feel as if someone's saying all of these things. In actuality, all that's happened is that the firm or individual you approached said no. Perhaps they hired someone else to do the job. Or the budget was unexpectedly cut and the project no longer exists. Or they decided to keep the work on the project internal. Or the person with whom you spoke about the project had a cat that just died.

In most cases, you won't know why your bid for work was rejected. That's why it's important not to take it personally. Rejection is an inevitable part of freelancing. The sooner you train yourself to accept it and move on, the sooner you'll be on the road to success.

Most of the time, the people rejecting your offer will be pleasant and professional. No one's going to scream. No one's going to question your talent. No one's going to tell you to get lost. You'll most likely be rejected very politely, or you'll never hear from the prospect at all.

Now how bad is that?

FREELANCER TIP

Try this exercise to help get over the fear of rejection. When one of your bids is rejected, sit in a comfortable chair, close your eyes, and whisper, "It's not personal." Repeat this ten times. Each time you say it, get in the habit of thinking what it could be:

It's not personal. There's no more money for it.

It's not personal. They just spilled coffee on their favorite shirt.

It's not personal. They changed bosses.

It's not personal. The transmission in their car died.

It's not personal. They changed their strategy.

Before long, it'll become a game—one you play whenever you've been told for the umpteenth, "Thank you for contacting us, but we have no need for your services at this time."

Focus on What You Offer

When you decide to freelance, you do so because you believe you have a product or service that will help others achieve their dreams. This product or service is unique to you, something you alone provide. It's something that solves someone else's problem.

It can be easy to lose sight of this when you're told, "Thanks, but no thanks." But it's important to hold on to this belief. It's what will keep you motivated to keep going.

An easy way to stay focused is to remember, "I have something valuable to offer. I design kick-ass websites that my clients love. Or, I write compelling copy that sells out seminars. Or, I write code that saves small business owners hundreds of man-hours in lost productivity."

Keep the focus on how what you offer helps potential clients achieve their objectives. When looked at this way, it's not about *selling* yourself; it's about *offering* solutions. Just ask yourself:

- What business wouldn't want to get a brand-spanking-new interactive website to replace that static one that's stuck in the nineties—the early nineties, no less?
- What entrepreneur wouldn't want sales copy that helps him go from holding seminars in a rented office that holds eight people to a seminar space with a 200-seat capacity?
- What cash-strapped start-up wouldn't want a custom program that allows them to access all their raw data at the click of a mouse, instead of having to dig through paper receipts (which your programming skills provided)?

You, my friend, are a problem solver.

Burn that message in your brain before you open your doors. Print it on a plaque and put it on your desk; write it on a Post-it and stick it on your laptop, tablet, or computer; have it painted and framed to hang on your office wall.

Whatever you need to do—remind yourself how awesome what you have to offer is. It'll make placing those sales calls so much easier and growing your business that much more fun.

Ask for Help

Just because you may work alone does not mean that you are alone. There are many organizations you can reach out to. Following are seven of the most practical and well regarded.

1. Freelancers Union

This national nonprofit organization represents the concerns of independent workers such as freelancers, consultants, and temps. It offers various forms of insurance to workers, as well as providing an advocacy platform and in-depth information on matters important to the freelance community. The organization is online at www.free lancersUnion.org.

2. Meetup.com

Meetup.com is the world's largest network of local groups. Freelance Meetups (www.meetup.com/topics/freelance) connects freelancers with other freelancers in their local area. You can start your own group or join an existing one in your niche in your area. Members can meet to network, discuss freelancing issues, barter, find a cowork space, or just to get out of the house and make new friends.

3. Small Business Administration (SBA)

This organization is a virtual treasure trove of information—everything from securing loans and contracts, to counseling and other forms of assistance. Log on to www.SBA.gov to learn more.

4. SCORE

SCORE is the acronym for Service Corps of Retired Executives. It is a nonprofit organization supported by the U.S. Small Business Administration (SBA) with a network of over 11,000 volunteers. It matches aspiring entrepreneurs with local volunteer mentors, and holds events and workshops via its 320-plus chapters, which are spread across the United States and its territories. SCORE's mentoring services are delivered at no charge, or at very low cost. SCORE is online at www.SCORE.org.

5. Small Business Development Centers (SBDCs)

There are nearly 1,000 service centers available to provide no-cost business consulting and low-cost training to aspiring entrepreneurs. SBDCs, funded in part by the U.S. Congress through a partnership with the SBA, are hosted by leading universities, colleges, and state economic development agencies. They provide free face-to-face business consulting and at-cost training in various areas such as how to write a proper business plan, securing start-up capital, and marketing. Find an SBDC near you at www.AmericasSBDC.org.

6. Chamber of Commerce

Many chambers of commerce have mentoring programs. Mentors are usually selected from professional connections they've developed within the chamber. The programs try to match business owners based on a variety of factors: educational background, type of business, personality, and potential worthwhile connections.

To find your local chamber, Google "chamber of commerce" and your city, state. Once you have their information, visit their website or call and ask them if they have a mentoring program. If they don't have one, check the largest city next to you. Sometimes, a small, local chamber might not have a mentoring program, but one in a larger metropolis will.

7. The Internet

Join some forums *in your niche*; follow the blogs of a few "gurus" *in your niche*; subscribe to industry-leading newsletters *in your niche*; stalk the social media accounts of those *in your niche*.

See the theme? Niche, niche, niche. Once you decide what type of freelance business you want to start, research people, institutions, publications, and organizations that are the movers and shakers in that niche—and learn from them.

As stated earlier, thanks to the web, there is practically always a way to find help to shed some light on whatever problem you're facing as a freelancer. Where possible, have a go-to person you can talk with when fear, doubt, and uncertainty threaten to overwhelm you. This can be anyone in your immediate circle who's supportive of your career choice, or a business mentor or coach.

Transitioning

"I quit!"

"I wish I could quit right now!"

"Man there's got to be more to life than this. I want to quit so bad."

"I like my job; I just wish it had more flexibility."

The decision to begin freelancing, as we've discussed, is a very important one. To make sure your freelance career gets off on the right foot, you need to think about exactly how you'll make this transition from working full-time for someone else to working on your own.

Some people do it responsibly—cleaning out their desk drawers, handing in their notices, and finger-biting those last two weeks on the job. Others do so with flair—walking into their boss's office, firmly stating, "I quit!" and never looking back. Still others squelch their desire for years—until they're fired, laid off, or have hours cut to the bone and are in effect pushed into freelancing.

Your entry into the freelance world doesn't have to be as dramatic. It can be smooth. Following are five things you can do to make the transition from a full-time job to freelancing full-time as joyful and successful as possible.

Start Planning Early

Start preparing for your exit from your job six months to a year out. This will give you plenty of time to think things through and put specifics in place to maximize your chance of success.

Reduce your monthly outlay as much as possible. Look at every expense, especially the biggies like rent or mortgage, car payments, and healthcare insurance. What can you reduce, get rid of, or switch to decrease your monthly expenses?

Don't leave anything on the table. If you're renting, would you consider moving to a cheaper apartment? How about getting a room-mate? What about selling your house and moving to a different, cheaper area if your freelance business is mobile? Everything should be up for consideration if you're serious about making a real go of freelancing.

Also, enlist the help and support of friends and family. Share with the important people in your life what your plan is. Your immediate circle is going to be impacted, so it might take some time for them to get used to it. By letting them know early, you give them a chance to adjust and get excited about this new chapter in all your lives.

Start Saving

Once you know what your monthly expenses are going to be, start saving your financial cushion. If you research how much you should save for your "freelance fund," you'll find figures quoted that advise anywhere from three months to a year of expenses. But it really is an individual decision. We'll talk more in Chapter 4 about creating an emergency fund.

Write Your Business Plan

Complete your business plan, as outlined in Chapter 3. This is your roadmap to freelance success. It ensures that you've thought of everything and are leaving nothing—nothing that is in your control, that is—to chance.

Acquire Clients

If you don't already have clients, start marketing for and landing clients. While doing all the upfront prep work will help you mitigate mistakes, there's nothing like on-the-job training for learning. Landing and completing jobs will give you a real idea of what your new career is going to be like. It's also a great confidence booster to have clients before you quit. It's proof that yes, indeed you can do this.

You're going to be sleepwalking into work some days. Get used to it, as you're in for quite a few long days as you juggle your new freelance career with your full-time job. But keep the end goal in mind and hold on to this: with more money coming in, you may be able to quit your full-time job sooner than you think.

Don't Burn Bridges

For many freelancers, their previous employer is one of their first clients. So don't burn any bridges. When the time comes, plan your exit from your job just as carefully and professionally as you've prepared to launch your freelance career.

What You've Learned

Are you getting excited? You should! A lot of ground has been covered. Here's a rundown of the things that should stand out to you.

- *It's an exciting time to freelance:* Remember, by 2020, a projected 40 percent of the American workforce (60 million) will be independent workers—freelancers, contractors, and temporary employees. More and more are choosing this lifestyle, and with good reason, as American businesses are increasingly turning to independent professionals to get work done.
- *Understand your why:* Have you figured out why you want to freelance yet? Remember, it will be your underlying motivation, so get very clear about why you want to make this exciting career change.
- *Habits of successful freelancers:* Remember those eight habits we discussed? How many of these do you have? Don't worry if you don't have all of them; they can be cultivated. Now that you know what they are, all you have to do is practice developing those you don't have.
- *Help is available:* There are people and organizations you can turn to for help—whether directly via a face-to-face mentoring program or virtually, by learning who the movers and shakers

are in your niche and staying up to date via their blogs, news-letters, websites, social media accounts, and so on.

- *Developing a freelance mindset:* Freelancing requires as much mental as physical preparation. The best part about this is, once you believe you can, the sky is literally the limit.

Chapter 2

What to Sell and What to Charge

So you've decided to freelance. Big sigh of relief.

Now all you have to do is decide exactly what it is that you're going to sell.

Decide What to Sell

Many freelancers start their freelance careers because there's something they've been doing on the side and it kind of morphs into a business. This is when panic can set in because you think, "Jeez, what else should I be offering?" Or "Is this one thing really enough to make a full-time go of freelancing?"

The following five questions will help you decide what products and/or services you should be offering.

What's Selling?

This is where you begin to investigate the competition (we'll talk more about that in Chapter 6). What services are most of them offering? This will give you a very good idea of what clients you want to target and are already paying others for.

What Are Your Talents?

Go with your strengths and your passions—and many freelancers have many more of these than they know. Following is an exercise that can help you ferret out all your talents, and offer products and services that play to your strengths.

This exercise involves mining your past to find out where your passions, experiences, hobbies, and desires can possibly intersect and form the basis for a viable list of services.

Degrees/ Specialized Skills I Have	Jobs I've Had	Things I'd Like to Do	Hobbies I've Had
MBA	Waitress	Live abroad	Martial arts
Bilingual (Italian)	Editor	Learn French	Wine making
Notary public	Mortgage consultant	Learn how to sail	Sewing

Let's say you have an MBA, but you have no desire to put that degree to use in corporate America. The idea of it makes you physically ill. However, you also want to travel, and you're bilingual (English/Italian).

You could start a freelance translation business, specializing in translating corporate documents. This will allow you to travel—to Italy perhaps—and maybe even get into wine making, since you'll be in the bosom of a wine-loving country.

See how helpful digging into your past can be?

How Do You Measure Up Against the Competition?

Don't psyche yourself out here. Many freelancers freak out when they start researching and looking at the competition on the web. The tendency is to think, "Man, I could never compete with them. Their website is awesome, and their brand is already so clearly defined. I'd just be wasting my time."

Stop!

Don't let this kind of restrictive thinking take over. Everyone has to start somewhere, and peripherals like getting a website are not as daunting as you may think. You only need to answer one question honestly here: Can I handle this job?

Don't get wigged out by the bells and whistles your perceived competition offers. Focus at this point on the product/service you can provide.

What Do You Enjoy?

Just because you're qualified to provide a service doesn't mean you should. If you thought working a nine to five that you hated was bad, wait until you freelance doing something you're not fond of because you thought it would be profitable—and instead of your regular paycheck from the company, there's $0 deposited at the end of the week.

That ain't no fun! So don't take this question lightly. Remember, there are a lot of unpaid hours in freelancing. Make sure you enjoy what you do. It'll make those weeks when you don't get paid much easier to swallow, and when you do get paid it'll make you feel like you hit the lottery.

What Are You Comfortable With?

Start off offering only the goods and services you're comfortable with, even if everyone else is offering a whole plethora of services. You're going to have enough on your plate when you first start. You don't want to get overwhelmed by trying to do too much too soon. You can always add on as you grow.

Pricing: Guidelines to Get It Right

If you want to break out in hives as a new freelancer, try to figure out what to charge. You want to find out what freelancers—normally a pretty level-headed, pleasant lot—fight about, start talking about rates. You want to find an excuse to take that extra tequila shot, try figuring out what to charge as a freelancer. Yeah, it's that bad. . . . But it doesn't have to be.

Whole books are written on how to price, but in the beginning keep it as simple as possible. Nothing is set in stone. You can always tweak your prices as you gain more experience.

Use the following simple formula to determine your rates. It will ensure that you don't set starving artist wages right out of the box, and that you won't want to shoot yourself in the head while trying to figure it out.

$$Costs + Profit = Rate$$

Determine Your Costs

Before you can begin to think about profit, you must first know how much it costs you to produce your product. We'll look more at this issue in the "Calculate Income Goals and Projections" section in Chapter 3.

Determine Your Profit

Once you know exactly how much it costs you to produce your product, then you can decide what a fair profit would be. When determining what your profit will be, don't forget to keep in mind your annual revenue target. In fact, this should be one of the primary factors you consider.

Some industries have standard, defined profit margins. For example, did you know that the cosmetics industry has some of the highest profit margins around—around 80 percent? No wonder it seems like every celebrity and her mother has a perfume line.

This is why setting prices can get sticky. You want to ensure that your profit margins are within industry standards while ensuring that you are not undercharging to the point where you can't afford to freelance; are not overcharging so that you price yourself out of the market; and can withstand the ups and downs of a changing economy.

So how do you achieve all of this? One way is to look to your competitors. Where available, comb through annual statements of small and midsized businesses in your niche, poke around in forums to see what the norms are, and check credible industry reports, analyses, and statistics.

It may take some digging, but you'll be able to see a trend—then determine where you'd like to fall in the pricing model.

Three Ways to Charge

A bunch of factors go into figuring out which method to use in charging, including your experience, your niche, your fixed costs, and your variable costs. Again, nothing is set in stone, especially in the beginning.

Following are three popular ways to charge. You may use one method with one client and another one with a different client, depending on the project. This is fine. The goal is to maximize your time, wringing the most profit out of each job that crosses your desk.

1. Hourly

This is a comfortable pricing model for many freelancers, especially for service-based businesses, because it's clearly defined for you and for the client. If you decide to use this method, be sure to include all the time you spend on a project, using productivity tools such as Toggl.

2. By the Project

Many clients prefer this method of pricing because they know exactly what your work is going to cost them. It can work to your advantage as a freelancer too, especially if you are intimately familiar with the job at hand and can turn it around quickly.

For example, if you're a freelance writer who specializes in personal finance content, you probably have a list of go-to resource links and industry organizations you can consult when you sit down to write an article. Also, because you write about this topic all the time, you already know what is pertinent to it. Hence, in forty-five minutes you can write a 700-word article on how to play catch-up when saving for retirement.

If your rate is $100 per hour, you earn $125 for that article if you charge a project rate. But, if you were new to the subject matter and it took you two or three hours to write the article, then your hourly rate is $33–$50.

So be careful if you decide to charge by the project. Make sure it's an industry you know really well so that you don't wind up making pennies, even though the project rate may seem like a lot.

3. Working on Retainer

This is a great way to build a long-term, repeat clientele. Landing just a few clients who pay you a set amount each month (that is, they keep you on retainer), can go a long way toward evening out the ups and downs of your freelance income.

Just like charging by the project though, you have to be careful here or you can find yourself becoming more like an employee instead of offering a business-to-business service.

Following are some factors to consider if you're considering offering this pricing model:

- Length of retainer agreement
- Exactly how many hours it covers
- Exactly what services are expected
- Exactly when the work is due
- Exactly when payment is due

Notice how the word *exactly* was repeated? That was not by accident. A retainer locks you in for a defined period of time, so you and the client must be on the same page about what is covered by your agreement and what's not.

If you're new to freelancing, try the hourly or project pricing models first. They're the easiest ones to start with and if you don't get the pricing right, you're not tied to a long-term agreement, which will allow you to adjust rates with your next project.

When the Client Sets the Rate

There will be times when the client sets the rate. At this point, you'll have to make a decision as to whether or not you want to take on the job. Following are three things to consider that will help you make an informed decision.

1. Does the job pay off in other areas? For example, is it with a high-profile client who could lead to other work?
2. Can you barter with the client? Does the client provide products and/or services that you need, can't afford, or have been on your wish list?
3. Is it something—for example, a charity—that would make you feel good?

Caution: Working for Less with the Promise of Future Work

One carrot that's frequently dangled in front of freelancers is, "If you do this for 'x,' then moving forward we'll be able to throw a lot more work your way."

Red alert. Red alert. Red alert. Rarely does this kind of arrangement work out. If a client has more work he could give you, he should be offering it to you right now, not at some distant point in the future. If he's not offering specifics for volume work that's available now or in the very near future—and isn't willing to sign a contract to that effect—then pass.

What You've Learned

Many freelancers get stuck in the start-up stage trying to figure out what to offer. That stumbling block can seem even higher once the

"What should I charge?" stage is reached. In this chapter, you gained concrete insight into:

- *How to decide what to offer:* The five questions outlined will give you a clear understanding of where your talents, strengths, and passions intersect, so you can offer products and/or services that play to your strengths.
- *What to do when a client can't afford you:* But you still might want to work with them.
- *How to figure out what to charge:* Keep it simple by using the "Costs + Profit = Rate" formula, especially in the beginning. This will allow you to easily see what your profit is, and whether or not you need to adjust rates. Remember, you can use all three of the formulas discussed, or just one. The key is to maximize income.

Now that you know how to overcome these two stumbling blocks, you're ready for the next phase of starting your freelance business—writing a business plan.

Chapter 3

Writing Your Business Plan

When you hear the words *business plan*, your first reaction may be to groan and think of a thirty-page document that required months of research and tons of hair pulling. Luckily, a freelance business plan doesn't have to be this.

Starting a business that will replace your job and allow you to live the type of life you've always dreamed of living is too important to just "wing it." You need a roadmap of how to get your freelance enterprise off the ground quickly, intelligently, and as cost-effectively as possible. And that's all a business plan is. It's your roadmap to freelance success.

The Most Important Thing

Every business has two types of customers: ideal and peripheral.

Ideal customers are loyalists. They are whom you do everything for. You craft your marketing messages for them; you create your products and services around them; you craft your brand and business identity around them. Your business exists to serve them and their needs.

Peripheral customers are those who patronize you because, for one reason or another, they stumble across you. They may buy from you if the price is right, if they like that particular color your product comes in, if they don't feel like going across town to that other store today. They're "iffy" customers.

Imagine you're a marathon runner. You've been running since you were in high school.

For your entire running career, you've been a Nike loyalist. Once, you tried another brand of running shoes because they were a birthday gift from a friend, but there wasn't enough support for your feet, even though they were new. They just never felt right. They sit in your closet and you use them on occasion to run weekend errands to the grocery store and the post office. When it's time to buy new running shoes, you don't even consider other brands because you know Nike. You know they will always be kind to your feet. They have never failed to provide the comfort you need as a runner. You, my friend, are a Nike loyalist.

This is the kind of customer you build a business and a brand around. Every decision—especially marketing, branding, and scaling—should be made with your *ideal customer* in mind, *not* peripheral ones.

With that in mind, let's talk about your business plan.

What a Traditional Business Plan Includes

There are many kinds of business plans. Some can run to 100 pages or more, while others can be as simple as five or ten pages. The length depends on a number of factors, primarily:

- The type of freelance business
- Your goals for it
- How you plan to accomplish those goals

Most traditional business plans can be broken down into four parts: executive summary; business concept; market analysis and marketing strategy; and financials. You're going to use this time-tested model to craft your business plan. This four-part structure ensures that you cover everything that's important, but without tearing your hair out. Here's what's covered in each of the business sections.

Executive Summary

This section is considered the most important section of a business plan. Think of it as a summary of all the other sections.

In this section, you'll find such details as what kind of business you have (e.g., products/services it provides), its location, its mission, number of employees, growth highlights, banking and other financial info.

FYI, when you're seeking outside financing, this is the first section investors peruse precisely because it's an overview of what's included in the overall plan. Although this section appears in the beginning of a business plan, it is usually the last section you'll write.

A Note about Executive Summaries

If you're reading this thinking, "Hmmm, is this section for freelancers or entrepreneurs? This sounds like a section for an entrepreneur to complete. Just what is the difference between an entrepreneur and a freelancer?"

As defined by Oxford Dictionaries, an entrepreneur is "A person who sets up a business or businesses, taking on financial risks in the hope of profit: many entrepreneurs see potential in this market." A freelancer is a person who works freelance, which Oxford Dictionaries says is "Self-employed and hired to work for different companies on particular assignments."

The key difference lies in how each approaches the economic market. Entrepreneurs look for gaps in the market, using their own or investor funds to fill a need. Freelancers look for already established markets in which to offer their goods and services, becoming a competitor in an existing, thriving marketplace.

While freelancers traditionally sell services such as web design and copywriting, they can offer products too. A freelance illustrator may create a line of T-shirts or prints to sell, while a freelance copywriter might self-publish a book. Freelancers can also hire others. For example, a web designer may hire a freelance writer to provide copy for all the websites she constructs. Freelancers usually only hire workers as independent contractors, as opposed to full-time or part-time employees, who are hired more by entrepreneurs.

As you can see, today's independent workers can successfully straddle the fence between freelancing and entrepreneurship. For the most part, freelancing is discussed in this book as it relates to independent workers who offer services, with the understanding that there can be some overlap with traditional small business entrepreneurship.

Business Concept/Company Description

This section provides specifics on your freelance business and what it does. Here, you'll cover such details as:

- The nature of your business and the niche you plan to cater to.
- Your specific plan for satisfying the pain points of your defined niche. In case you don't know, a pain point is a problem—real or perceived—that a potential client has that you seek to solve via your product or service offering.
- Your unique selling point (USP). You'll also see this referred to as a unique selling proposition. Either way, what it's referring to is what makes your freelance business different and/or better than the competition. We'll discuss how to craft a USP in Chapter 6.
- Any other competitive advantages you bring to the table.
- Where you're located.

Market Analysis and Marketing Strategy

This part of your business plan—discussed in detail in this chapter—builds on the previous section by offering a detailed overview of the niche you intend to service, including statistical analyses that back up your claims. Here you'll also discuss why your USP is viable, including how you will price, promote, and market your product or service.

Financials

This section covers how you'll finance your freelance business, including but not limited to: what you'll need for start-up; how you'll cover day-to-day operating expenses; and what will be needed for future growth.

Refining the Plan

In writing your freelance business plan, you have some advantages over many small businesses:

- You know what your business concept is
- You're probably not seeking financing (at least not at this point)

Hence, you won't need a lot of what goes into a traditional business plan. Your primary focus at this point is having a well-thought-out plan you can follow that will help you succeed. You'll also change the order a bit from the structure I outlined in the previous section. Here are the issues you'll need to address.

Market Analysis

Most business plans start with an executive summary or the business concept. The reason market analysis is listed as the first section in your freelance business here is that it will give you a whole bunch of insight into what's possible—and what's not—in your targeted niche.

After all, that's what marketing is about. You start with an idea, then look for evidence to support that it's a viable idea, right?

The reason so many freelance businesses fail is because many people never take the time to do an in-depth market analysis. You may find that your idea should have just remained a side gig, or that you should have gone in a different, more profitable, direction. One good place to start your market analysis is with other freelancers in your targeted niche. Ask them questions such as:

- What services are they offering?
- How much are they charging?
- How long have they been in business?
- Who are their customers?
- How are they reaching those customers?
- How are they different from your business?

After you've done your market analysis, then you can move on to the next step.

Define Your Brand

What's your freelance business's message? What's your brand? Everything you do—marketing, scaling, determining your USP, etc.—will flow from this, so you need to be really clear about what this is.

What Is a Brand?

The official definition of *branding* according to www.Business Dictionary.com is:

The process involved in creating a unique name and image for a product in the consumers' mind, mainly through advertising campaigns with a consistent theme. Branding aims to establish a significant and differentiated presence in the market that attracts and retains loyal customers.

Well-defined brands are easily recognizable, just from a slogan or logo; buyers know what to expect from them, and the message is consistent. A concise example of a clearly defined brand is Nike. You see the swoosh, and you know it's Nike. You hear the phrase, "Just Do It!" and you instantly think of Nike. And you know they sell sporting goods and apparel. This is because: their message is consistent; their slogan is memorable; their logo is instantly recognizable; and you can sum up their business in a few seconds.

This is no accident. These are the exact elements that it takes to create a successful brand, and why it's so important to get really clear about what yours will be early on. We'll discuss how to create a successful brand in detail in Chapter 5.

Calculate Income Goals and Projections

Another grave mistake many freelancers make is not knowing how to do financial projections and set proper income goals. For example, many will make replacing their current income their initial financial goal. This is great, especially if what you're earning is what you need—at a minimum—to meet your current monthly obligations. But your paycheck includes so much more than the dollars deposited into your account.

Statistics from the Bureau of Labor Statistics (BLS) show that employer-paid benefits are a pretty good chunk of your overall salary. Just how much?

- Employer costs for employee compensation for civilian workers averaged $33.37 per hour worked in September 2015. Wages and salaries averaged $22.88 per hour worked and accounted for 68.6 percent of these costs, while benefits averaged $10.48 and accounted for the remaining 31.4 percent.
- Total employer compensation costs for private industry workers averaged $31.53 per hour worked in September 2015. Benefits averaged $9.55 per hour, which accounted for 30.3 percent of costs.

Some common things included in an employee benefit package that the vast majority of freelancers don't have access to include vacation days, sick days, retirement/pension contributions, and family leave.

FREELANCER TIP

Family leave is huge. In case you don't know, this benefit is formally called the Family and Medical Leave Act (FMLA). It's a federal law that guarantees certain employees up to twelve workweeks of unpaid leave each year, with no threat of job loss. FMLA also requires employers to continue to cover employee health benefits, just as if they were still working.

When you're doing the financial projections for your freelance business, these costs must be taken into account to accurately reflect what you need to earn to cover your existing salary if that is your marker.

This is why it pays to get out of as much debt as you can before you start freelancing. This way, when you're determining financial projections and setting income goals, even if you're earning less, you'll be able to afford your lifestyle while you build your business.

Making a Projected Income Statement

An income statement is a report that shows the profit and losses of a business. It is commonly referred to as a profit and loss (P&L) statement. Another way you may hear it referred to is "statement of revenues and expenditures" (usually government entities call it that). An income statement contains a company's revenue, expenses, and gains and losses for a defined period (e.g., a month, a quarter, a year). The beauty of an income statement is that you can look at it and get a snapshot of the entity's financial health.

Generating a projected income statement will keep you focused on your financial goals month after month. This is extremely important—especially when you first start. With that first one under your belt, you'll be excited to look back over your number each month to see how you're doing. At the end of year, you'll know exactly what you need to do to stay on track for success.

Even if you don't have any actual sales numbers when you first start out, you should still generate an income statement because if you've done your research, there are some fixed costs that you will be able to account for: your phone service, Internet, cost to rent a coworking space, how much you've budgeted to market initially, and so on.

Projected income statements—like all matters in finance—can be as simple or complicated as you want. To start with, though, you just need a basic statement. Here is what should be included on it. Following is what a six-month projected income statement looks like.

Following the table is an explanation of the categories.

MY FREELANCE BUSINESS
PRO FORMA INCOME STATEMENT

SALES	MONTH 1	MONTH 2	MONTH 3	MONTH 4	MONTH 5	MONTH 6
Biz Clients						
Individuals						
Gross Sales Income						
Materials						
Overhead						
Labor						
Taxes						
Cost of Goods Sold						
GROSS PROFIT						
PROFIT PERCENT						

Sales/Gross Sales Income

If you're just starting out, you won't have anything to put here, of course. Instead, guesstimate how much income you expect to earn. While it's not necessary to segment your customers into categories like "Biz Clients" and "Individuals," you might want to get in the habit of doing so. Why? Because when you do start to land clients, you will be able to record the profit (or loss) from each sector. This will allow you to fine-tune your marketing efforts to land more of the types of clients who are profitable, and to stop wasting time on those who aren't.

Cost of Goods Sold

If you operate a product-based freelance business, this is relatively easy to figure out because you can point to a cost of raw goods that you buy from a manufacturer. But remember, the vast majority of freelance businesses are service-based enterprises, so there would be no cost of "goods" sold, which makes this category a bit more sticky.

The Small Business Administration (SBA) has one of the most straightforward, clear explanations of how to treat this category—whether it's a service-based or product-based business. It advises you to take the following factors into consideration when setting rates, which help determine income and expenses:

- Materials
- Overhead
- Labor

There's one more you should take into account as well—taxes.

Materials cost. These are the costs of goods you incur in providing the service. Most freelance businesses, because they're service-based, won't have this cost, but there are some exceptions. For example, if you operate a pet-sitting service, some essential pet-sitting business supplies include pet first-aid kits, spare collars and leashes, towels and blankets, and pet treats and toys.

Overhead costs. In this column list all indirect costs you incur in running your freelance business. These include rent, utilities, marketing, taxes, office supplies, insurance, and administrative expenses (e.g., if you have an administrative assistant or office manager).

Labor costs. This is the cost of any direct labor you hire to provide the service. Using the pet-sitting business example, this would be the cost of dog walkers or cat sitters whom you hire on a contract basis.

To make this distinction clear, think of it this way—an administrative assistant helps to run your entire freelance business. That's why this type of labor cost is under overhead as an indirect cost. A direct labor cost is anyone you hire to actually provide the service you're performing.

What about your own labor? Good question. A big mistake many freelancers make is not accounting for their own time when considering business expenses—and this should be perhaps one of your biggest costs—your own salary. A big part of the reason many freelancers don't classify their own labor as a cost is that the IRS defines a freelancer's salary as any net profit their business makes. So in this sense, your labor is not a "cost."

However, it's your job to ensure that you do receive compensation, and you can do so by paying yourself a fixed salary. This will force you to do things such as: really assess the types of clients you want to target; set living-wage rates from the beginning; maintain your cash flow; and follow up on overdue accounts.

Accounting for Your Income on an Income Statement

You can set up your income statement any way you want, as long as you remain in compliance with IRS guidelines, which again, counts any profits from your freelance efforts as your income/salary.

If you decide to pay yourself a salary, you can put it on your income statement as an "Owner's Draw" for example. As long as you account for it and pay taxes on it, that's all the IRS cares about.

The structure of your business, whether it's a sole proprietorship or a corporation, becomes important in terms of tax breaks, how your income is declared, and other factors, once you start talking salary. This is one reason you may want to consult an accountant, so you'll know exactly what your options are, and how to ensure that you get paid regularly.

Taxes. Many freelance businesses overlook tax expenses. Be sure to know the tax laws as they pertain to your business so you're always in compliance. If you fail to follow tax laws, you may be subject to civil and/or criminal penalties.

FREELANCER TIP

This calculation can tell you if expenses are getting out of hand. If you generated $50,000 in revenue, but your gross profit was only 40 percent ($20,000) and this is not in line with the standard in your industry, you may start looking for ways to cut expenses. For example, maybe move the business into your home instead of paying for that coworking space.

If you let the coworking space go, which is costing you $250 per month ($3,000) per year, it will boost your gross profit by 6 percent immediately, and it's really more than that because if you have a dedicated space in your home for your business, you can claim a home office deduction when you file taxes.

Add up all the monthly projection figures and you'll have a very clear picture of what you need to do to hit your financial goals.

Knowing Your Numbers—It Literally Pays

After reading this section, you may be thinking, "I'm hiring a CPA. I can't, I just can't do this!"

While it's great to have a professional to have onboard from day one, you should always know your numbers. This is not some data that you leave tucked away with your accountant.

To know your numbers is to know your business. Without focusing on them, you can't possibly know what's working, what's not, what needs to be changed, and how to grow your freelance business. It's why so many freelancers live a feast-or-famine existence. They have no clue about their numbers—until tax time rolls around each year.

Don't fall victim to this way of operating. Successful freelancers know their numbers. It's why they're able to continue to live the dream, instead of having to go back to a nine-to-five job they may hate.

Your Marketing Strategy

You've completed your market analysis. You've defined your brand. You know what financial goals you want to reach. Now, it's time to get down to the nitty-gritty of how you're going to get clients flowing through the door. Your marketing strategy should include the following three elements:

1. Number of Clients You Need to Land Each Month

This is why it's important to do an annual financial projection. It will help you determine how many clients you need to be landing month in and month out, and how much, on average, you need them to spend with you to meet your financial goals.

2. How Many Touches You Will Make Every Day/Week

In sales jargon, a touch refers to any time you reach out to a prospect. It can be in the form of a cold call, an e-mail, a direct message (DM) on social media, or a postcard mailer. Marketing is a numbers game, and the more touches you make, the more likely you are to get a sale.

In the beginning, you won't have much to go on, which makes it all the more important that you track results. So if you start out by saying, "I'm going to make five cold calls a day," and you do that for a month and you land two new clients, then you can say you have a 2 percent conversion rate with cold-calling (five calls per weekday times four weeks equals 100 calls per month).

By contrast, if you mail out 100 postcards and land one client, that's a 1 percent response rate. Now, this could still be a successful marketing campaign—if that one client spends enough with you to cover the cost of that mailer, and especially if she goes on to become a repeat client. So it's not about how much you spend (as long as it is within your budget, of course), it's about the return on investment (ROI).

After a few months, you'll start to get an idea of expected results: If I make ten cold calls per weekday, that's 200 per month. If I get a 2 percent return rate, I'll be landing four new clients per month. And if I keep up with my postcard marketing campaign, doubling that too, then that's two more new clients I can expect. So just by mailing out 200 postcards per month and making ten cold calls per day, I can expect to land six new clients per month on average.

You'll find that this number may waver—sometimes you'll get more, sometimes you'll land less, but it's all about an average. If a particular marketing method works, keep using it. Never stop doing what's working, until the numbers tell you not to.

Successful salesman have a saying: "Every no gets you closer to a yes."

3. How You Are Going to Reach Clients

One of the questions you should have answered during your market analysis is where your clients are—both online and off? If you know they hang out in LinkedIn forums, join and participate. You should have multiple ways to reach your target audience. Your marketing calendar may look something like this:

- 7 A.M.: Mail out ten postcards (to stay on track of monthly goal of 200)—you want to make sure these are in the box first thing so you don't miss the postman.
- 7:30–8:30: Participate in LinkedIn forum. Be sure to reach out to at least five new contacts (decision-makers).
- 8:30–9:30: Make ten cold calls.

- 9:30–10: Break (celebrate sticking to the cold-call routine).
- 10–11: Work on proposal for one client who was interested when I called (yes!).

You may have noticed that all of these marketing activities take place during morning hours. Do your marketing first because without it, there will be no clients, and without clients, there's no business. Hence, *nothing else is more important than marketing*. It's the lifeblood of your business.

FREELANCER TIP

It's the most important question you'll ask clients who call you. "How did you hear about me/us?"

Tape a note to your computer, have it engraved on a plaque for your desk, wear a blue ribbon around your wrist—whatever it is, have some way to remind yourself to ask clients how they found you when they first contact you.

You may have sources out there working for you that you had no idea about (e.g., you are mentioned in a forum, quoted in an article on a popular blog, or show up in search results). Knowing where your leads are coming from is like knowing who's depositing money into your bank account. It's that important, so stay on top of it.

Set a defined marketing budget. If you don't have the template to create one, use free ones, which you can find online. Cold-calling wigs out a lot of people, but it's free (assuming you already have a phone), and it can be highly effective. There's also e-mail. There's never an excuse not to market.

Analyze your results. This is the only way to know if what you're doing is working or not working at all. Record your daily marketing

activities, then at the end of each month, go back and tally up what
they netted you. Some metrics to measure are:

- How many new clients did you land?
- Which marketing methods brought in the most leads/projects?
- What types of services are selling the most?
- How many queries did you receive from prospective clients?
- How much did you earn?

There are many more factors you'll be considering as your business grows, of course, but keeping an eye on these will allow you to
figure out what marketing methods are working the best, what services you may need to add, what type of client you're attracting, and
what you need to do to increase income.

Marketing Tips

Marketing is a complicated business, but you'll get better at it
with experience. Here are some things to think about when you're
considering particular marketing techniques:

- *Can you afford it:* Only engage in marketing activities you can
  afford to repeat. This is because the effectiveness in marketing
  can only be found in repetition. So while you may be able to
  run a cost-per-click (CPC) Google ad campaign this month, is
  it something you can afford to do every month? If you can't,
  then don't.
- *Repetition is key:* When you're thinking of marketing, write
  down every conceivable kind of marketing you can think of
  that will reach your target market. Then, choose the two or
  three you know you will consistently do to start with.
- *Keep a calendar:* A marketing calendar will allow you to see
  exactly what you should be doing day in and day out. Time-
  block it as mentioned previously. This way, you'll be tied to

a specific time for each activity, making it much more likely you'll get to it, because then you'll get to scratch that off your list for the day.

- *Marketing never stops:* When was the last time you saw a McDonald's ad on television? How about an ad for a new car by Ford or Chevrolet or Mercedes? How about one for a mega bank? Most likely, it was recently. The point? Marketing never stops. You think everybody doesn't already know what McDonald's is, or Ford, or Bank of America? Of course they do. But the companies are still buying those mega-expensive television ads. The advertising is still on your car radio, still on billboards when you drive down the interstate. It's because those companies want to stay top of mind with you, so when you're in the market for what they offer, you think of them first.

This is one reason continuous marketing is necessary. As your freelance business grows, you'll find that more of your projects will come via referral. But even in that case, never stop marketing. While your clients may be as loyal as the day is long, if you're not staying in touch with them and reaching out to new ones, one day you'll look up and wonder what happened to the thriving enterprise you were on your way to building.

Final Issues to Consider When Writing Your Business Plan

Whew, you did it! You finished your business plan. While it is a lot of work, it's one of the best investments in your freelance business you can ever make. In fact, it's priceless, so celebrate this achievement, knowing that you've done what the vast majority of freelancers never do, which makes your success that much more likely.

A couple of final things to think about:

1. Does your freelance business require some kind of special zoning and/or licensing if you're working from home?
2. If you're working from home, does your homeowners insurance cover accidents that may occur when/if contractors and/or employees visit/consult with you there?
3. Do you have a dedicated space for your business in your home, which can be used as a tax write-off?
4. Do any rules (e.g., condo association or homeowners association) prevent you from using your home for commercial enterprises? Be sure to check your covenants or statutes.
5. If you're using outside help, are they independent contractors (1099 workers) or employees? Get clear on this because it can cost you big with the IRS if you don't. See this section of the IRS's site to determine if the person you hire is an independent contractor or an employee. If you're still not sure, be sure to contact a licensed CPA.

Chapter 4

Start-Up Costs

"Yes!"

You've decided to go for it. You know you're not alone. You know where to turn for help when and if you need it. You've taken heed of the advice about how to successfully transition from your full-time job. Now you're really ready to step out on your own and start your freelance business.

Congratulations!

Deciding is one of the hardest parts of this career choice. Why? Remember when we talked in Chapter 1 about mentally preparing to freelance? You're going to find that 90 percent of the challenges you face when you freelance are mental. That's freeing in a way because once you realize this, you can find the right mindset and then get on with the specifics. One of the first specifics you'll tackle is the cost associated with starting.

Categorizing Your Start-Up Costs

How much your start-up costs are depends on what type of freelance business you're starting. The more complex your freelance plans, the greater your costs. Following are seven categories of expenses.

Breaking down your costs this way will help you calculate exactly what you need and how much it's going to cost.

1. Communication Expenses

Today's technology makes it very easy—and cheap—to connect with other people, whether they're clients or resources. The first expense in this category, of course, is an Internet connection. You need it to do things like Skype with clients—and Skype is free.

In addition to Skype, you can communicate with other people in some of the following ways:

E-Mail

This is mostly free, but there are circumstances in which it can cost. For example, if you're going to freelance in the area of graphic design, you're most likely going to be sending and receiving large files, which can't be sent via e-mail. You'll need to sign up for a service such as Dropbox.

In case you don't know, Dropbox is a virtual storage solution for photos, videos, docs, and other files. So if you need to send a client a large file that can't be sent or accessed via e-mail, you can store it via Dropbox and have your client access it there.

Dropbox allows files to be shared with anyone via a link; the link can be shared via multiple mediums, such as Facebook, Twitter, instant message, social networks, and so on.

Dropbox has free and paid accounts. Paid subscriptions currently start at $9.99/month.

Phone

This is where costs can escalate, particularly if you have a client who lives in another country. If you need to talk directly to a client in another country and need to do it a lot, there are many cheap or free alternatives to the telephone, such as Skype. However, some of the people with whom you deal may be stuck in their ways and not up on technology. They either want to meet you in person or talk to you on the phone. If this is the case, your phone bill can escalate quickly.

FREELANCER TIP

One of the wonderful things about freelancing is that you get to decide how you run your business. If you have a policy of not meeting in person, you can say no. If the client insists, you'll have to decide if she is worth it.

2. Office Supplies and Equipment

The basic stuff you need includes:

- A computer (desktop, laptop, or tablet, etc.)
- A printer, copier, and scanner (the all-in-one machine versions are very economical and probably the one you need)
- Office chair(s)
- Desk
- Tables
- Office supplies: toner/ink, paper, paper clips, pens, pencils, scissors, stapler, folders, etc.
- Software: MS Office Suite, which contains most of the common programs most use frequently (i.e., MS Word, PowerPoint, and Excel); anti-virus protection such as Norton; QuickBooks (accounting software); Carbonite (file storage software); and any other software you purchase to complete projects
- Miscellaneous: This includes things like trade stock accounts; for example, if you're a graphic designer, you might need to pay for a Shutterstock account to get photos for client websites

The good news about these start-up costs is that, for the most part, the most expensive items only need to be renewed annually and/or replaced every few years—for example, your computer.

3. Work Space

Many freelancers work out of home offices. That's great and gets you a tax deduction. However, freelancing can be isolating. Working by yourself with no contact with the outside world other than e-mail can depress you. For this reason, many freelancers choose to use cowork spaces.

These are spaces shared by people from different organizations and professions. Often, the spaces are outfitted with all the equipment you would find in a regular office: printers, copiers, scanners, and access to conference rooms. In many cases, you can rent these spaces by the hour, day, month, and even by the year.

According to Hera Hub in an article titled "Why Coworking?," what makes coworking so popular is that "It provides independent workers a place to get work done, meet clients and professionally 'show up,' both mentally and physically. Coworking also provides a social environment where individuals can work independently while still being part of a community of talented individuals with shared values and synergy."

How Much Do They Cost?

According to research published in 2014 by Cowork|rs, a New York workspace, the average cost of a dedicated desk—the kind you can scatter your stuff on and be confident it won't be disturbed—is $526 a month in New York. In San Francisco, it's slightly higher at $570. In Boulder, Colorado, it's $350. In Austin, Texas, $200 is the average monthly cost for a coworking space. As with everything in real estate, it's all about location, location, location. The cost will vary based on where you live—and what facilities you're seeking.

Home Office

If you decide to go the home office route, where possible, dedicate a room in your home as your office. The main reason is, you qualify for tax write-offs.

The Internal Revenue Service (IRS) is very strict about what qualifies as a home office, so be careful before making this deduction. A home office, the IRS, says, is an area used "exclusively and regularly as your principal place of business." That means you can't also use it for personal stuff; it's *only* for business.

It's pretty easy to pass the exclusivity test and write off certain home expenses such as mortgage and rent payments, homeowners or renters insurance, the cost of utilities, and even direct upkeep costs associated with that defined space (e.g., painting the walls or repairing the floor). It's deductions like these that send many freelancers running to professional tax preparers.

4. Professional Fees

The following types of fees fall into this category.

Accountant

To prepare your taxes or—depending on the size of your freelancing business—to help out with bookkeeping, you might hire an accountant.

FREELANCER TIP

Although hiring an accountant is probably the safest way to prepare your taxes, if you want to save money there are plenty do-it-yourself options such as TurboTax and Quicken. These will walk you step by step through your taxes to make sure you get every possible deduction. It just takes a bit of patience.

Attorney

It's a good idea to retain a lawyer to look over contracts. Also, you can pay one to create boilerplate legal templates of contracts for your business, contracts you can use over and over again.

Just as with a cowork space, you can save money here by using the services of a "co-op" legal service such as LegalShield (formerly Pre-Paid Legal Services). For the monthly cost of a lunch, you can have an attorney look over a legal document, write a letter on your behalf, or get legal advice. You can also consult sites such as www .LegalZoom.com, www.LawHelp.org, www.Nolo.com, and www .ProBono.net to find an attorney.

Training, Licensing, and Professional Development

This important category can range from renewing licenses, to getting trained to provide a specific service.

Membership and/or Association Fees

Membership in professional organization is important, since it allows you to effectively network and expand your client list. As well, you learn about the latest developments in your field, which makes you more employable.

5. Travel

Any travel you do that is primarily for business purposes is tax deductible. These can add up when you file your taxes, so be sure to keep receipts. Travel deductions include, but are not limited to:

- Travel, including plane fare, car rental fees, cruise tickets, taxis, and car service fees
- Lodging
- Meals

These are the most obvious fees associated with travel. Here are some often-overlooked expenses in this category (these are also deductible):

- Parking fees, whether in town, at the airport, or hotel valet
- Baggage fees charged by airlines

- Dry cleaning and laundry when you are traveling
- Incidental expenses, including tips to porters, baggage carriers, hotel staff, and staff on ships; computer rental fees; notary fees (if you're on the road and need to get a document notarized); and communication fees (e.g., faxes and international calls)

Consult IRS Publication 463 for a complete list of deductible travel expenses for self-employed individuals.

FREELANCER TIP

For many freelancers, combining work and pleasure is part of what makes freelancing such an ideal career. When you're freelancing, though, be careful not to run afoul of IRS guidelines.

For example, if you take a business trip to Hawaii and decide to stay three extra days for some fun in the sun, you can't deduct the cost of your hotel and meals for those three days. You can, however, still deduct the full cost of the airfare—because your primary reason for taking the trip was for business.

6. Petty Cash

The amount you'll need in your petty cash fund will depend on your type of freelancer business. For some, $25 is adequate. For others, the amount may be a couple of hundred. It should be small enough so that it doesn't tie up needed company assets but large enough to cover unexpected small purchases. Some things you'll spend petty cash on include:

- Postage
- Food/drink/entertainment
- Local travel, whether by car or public transportation

While a couple of hundred dollars tucked away for incidental expenses like this may seem like a little thing, it's not. It creates financial discipline. If you can't manage small amounts of money, you'll probably have difficulty with large amounts.

7. Emergency Fund

Industry-accepted wisdom is to save three to nine months' worth of living expenses before you start freelancing. This includes enough to cover all your bills—not just the big-ticket expenses like rent and/ or mortgage. Can you start to freelance with less? Absolutely. It all depends on your risk tolerance.

This is personal and depends on a host of different factors: what your parents taught you about money; how you handle money; how much debt you have; and what you need to feel secure.

For example, if you grew up in a household where money was always tight, your risk tolerance may be high because you're used to somehow "making things work." Conversely, it may make you more averse to risk, which means having a larger emergency fund.

To help you decide exactly how much you'll need, keep the following four things in mind:

1. Do you have children and/or dependents to support?
2. If so, does/will your spouse/mate contribute financially? How much?
3. Will you continue to work either full-time or part-time?
4. How much debt do you have?

FREELANCER TIP

When it comes to risk, listen to your gut. If you feel that you need at least $10,000 in an emergency fund to feel comfortable, but you run the numbers and can get by on $5,000, continue to save until you reach $10,000. You'll feel much less stressed when you start your freelance career because your *instinctual* financial needs are covered.

Things That Can Wait

If you're new to freelancing, your first instinct may be to walk into Staples or IKEA and stock up on all the latest in computer equipment, printers, cushy chairs, cool desks, and thingamabobs to decorate your cool new desk.

Don't. Stop!

Ask yourself, "If a potential client was ready to hire me today, what would I absolutely need to get the job done?" This is the only question you need to answer to figure out exactly what you need to get started right now.

Yes, starting a freelancing career is exciting. But when you first start out, the only things you need are those it takes to get a job done *today*. That's it and nada más, okay?

"But I have some start-up capital," you may be thinking. "I can afford it."

Great! Save it for a rainy day because in freelancing there will always be dry spells. Then you'll be glad for the extra cushion.

Two Advantages of Starting with Just the Basics

After you get the absolute necessities out of the way, let the other stuff go for a while. Think of it as putting your dreams on layaway—purchasing them a little at a time with each new project that comes in. There are two advantages to doing this:

1. It will allow you to get a feel for freelancing. Once you do and you get that cash in hand, you may say to yourself, "It took a month to land that client and two more months to finish the job and get paid for it. That was three months with no money coming in; I'm glad I didn't buy that expensive desk. The one I had in the garage works just fine."
2. It gets you in the habit of practicing fiscal responsibility, which will make you successful that much sooner when you freelance.

Three Things to Remember

By breaking down your start-up costs into categories, you can more easily assess what you need right now, and what can wait until later. Following are three things to keep in mind as you tally your start-up costs.

1. Get Out of Debt

Get out of debt as much as possible before you start to freelance. Some financial experts advise freelancers to only get in one kind of debt—mortgage. For many, this is unrealistic, especially if you're saddled with huge student loan debt. But paying off consumer debt like credit cards and a car note (which lowers your insurance rate) might be achievable.

2. Manage Your Money

Get intimate with your money. As a freelancer you're responsible for every penny you bring in, from deciding what to spend on office supplies to paying self-employment taxes. These are things you probably never had to think about before.

You work hard for your money. Make it work hard for you too by not wasting it. Know where it's going by getting in the habit of tracking it.

3. Comparison Shop

The Internet makes this very easy to do. Source everything before you plunk down one penny. This includes every cost from big expenses, such as coworking spaces, to little ones, such as which type of ink cartridge to buy for your printer.

Again, every penny you spend is money you worked hard for. Get the best value for your buck by doing some comparison shopping. Search for coupons. You can do this easily by going to your favorite search engine and typing in "online coupons for (name, product, and/or store)." You'd be amazed at how many deals retailers offer that aren't widely advertised.

Don't be afraid to negotiate. It's a skill you need to develop as a freelancer anyway. Ask, and you just may receive.

What You've Learned

To recap, in this chapter we've covered:

- *Breaking down expenses:* How to determine and categorize start-up costs
- *Work space costs:* What home office IRS deductions are, and which ones you can legally take
- *Professional fees:* Professionals you might want to consult to help get you up and running (e.g., a lawyer, an accountant, etc.)
- *Travel deductions:* How to account for expenses when you combine business and pleasure
- *Emergency funds:* The importance of creating an emergency fund, including how to determine how much you'll need in yours

As you can see, starting up is a bit more involved than buying supplies and hanging out your freelance shingle. The more particulars you address in the start-up phase, the greater your chance of freelance success. So confront each one head on. You'll feel so much more prepared when you open your doors.

Chapter 5

Building a Brand on a Shoestring Budget

What would you think if your friend asked you, "Let's grab lunch at the golden arches?" You'd think of McDonald's, right?

How about the expression, "Just do it!" Nike, right?

And "'Finger-lickin' good"? KFC's exploded in your head.

This is the power of branding.

Multibillion-dollar companies like the ones mentioned didn't start out that way. Their brands were built from the ground up, just like you're going to do. In Chapter 3 we briefly referred to branding. Now we're going to look at how to construct a brand for your freelance business.

Three Keys to Branding Success

Following are the only three things you need to focus on to bootstrap your way to branding success.

1. Your Message

All elements of your branding campaign start with your company message. So even though you may be selling web design services, that's not what your freelance business *is*. It's about helping entrepreneurs make their dream come alive right before their eyes. It's about making them feel confident that what they're offering is necessary, wanted, and needed. It's about transforming the vision they have in their head into a tangible business that customers will beat down their door for.

This is what you're selling; not a simple website.

When you're confident, anything is possible.

See how important it is to get laser-focused on your message? Until this is crystal clear, you can't do anything else in the branding process. Here are some questions to ask that will help crystallize your branding message:

- What is your ideal customer?
- Who are their heroes; what do they believe in?
- What does your brand believe in as it relates to them and their beliefs/heroes?
- What primary purpose does your freelance business serve for them?

These questions will help you clarify exactly what your business is all about, how it connects with its primary customers, and how it's different from others. This is at the heart of your unique selling point, which I mentioned earlier.

2. Your Slogan

Did you know that the word *slogan* derives from a Gaelic term employed by Scottish Highlanders as a war cry? That's a good way to think of this marketing term today—as your battle cry. It should be a message you can get across quickly. Remember, you're in battle; this is no time to be peaceful.

Remember Burger King's "Have it your way" slogan?

How about Coke's "Have a coke and a smile"?

L'Oréal's "Because you're worth it"?

Perhaps one of the funniest of all time: Wendy's "Where's the beef?"

Even when the name of the company (or even the product or service) is not part of it, you can instantly associate that brand with its slogan.

Notice how each one sums up what the product/service is all about—with benefit to the customer hinted at, overtly or covertly? This is what makes a great slogan.

Many companies keep their slogans for years; some never change them. When developing yours, think long term, say five or ten years. While there may come a time when your freelance business needs to change its slogan, you should start out with one you think you can grow with for a few years.

Elements of a Great Slogan

It's short. It should roll off the tongue. Shorter phrases make this easier. Note: There are exceptions to this; for example, NyQuil's slogan, "The nighttime, sniffling, sneezing, coughing, aching, stuffy head, fever, so you can rest medicine." There is no way in heck you should be able to recite this, but you know many people can! It's because NyQuil's marketed it up the wazoo.

It's memorable. It should make you remember the product or service. You can have the cleverest slogan around, but if prospects can't remember the name of your company, product, or service when they hear it, it doesn't mean a hill of beans. It's like being famous, but broke. Your goal is to make money, not just to be known for the sake of being known.

It's benefits oriented. The foundational message of a slogan is this is what's in it for you.

- Burger King's "Have it your way": The benefit is you're not stuck with number 7 from the menu. You can be different.
- Coke's "Have a coke and a smile": They're not selling a soft drink; they're selling happiness. Smile. It's all good.

- L'Oréal's "Because you're worth it": This is one of the most blatant slogans around—they flat out tell you, you're valuable honey. You're worth it!
- Wendy's "Where's the beef?": The underlying benefit is that you get more for your money with us.

So make it short, make it memorable, and appeal to the "What's in it for me" (WIIFM) feelings we all have, and you'll have a great slogan.

A slogan works in conjunction with a logo to promote brand identity. Once you've clarified your message and worked out what your slogan is going to be, it's now time to relay that message visually in the form of a logo.

3. Your Logo

Once your logo is created, it's going to serve as the foundation of your brand because it's going to go everywhere—on your website, blog, social media accounts; in your newsletter; in your marketing materials—everywhere. So take some time to really consider what you want this to be and if it gets across your core message and supports your slogan.

Spending money on branding in general and this aspect of branding in particular is some of the best money you can spend as you grow your freelance business. Hence, if this is all new to you, consult some experts.

Creating the Perfect Logo

- *Use original art:* Clip art is too obvious and it cheapens your business. Fortunately these days, logos don't have to cost a fortune. There are many online outlets that specialize in creating logos, including creating original art.
- *Make it appropriate to your niche/business:* While your logo may not convey exactly what you do, it shouldn't mislead your

customer. If you're a freelance writer, an image of a quill or a computer is great; an image of, say, a beer bottle, not so much.

- *Make it timeless:* Like your slogan, you want a logo that you're unlikely to outgrow in a few years. So resist trendy images and fads. Stick to timeless, classic images—and this doesn't have to mean boring. Classic means always in style, and that can still be fun and hip.
- *It should be clean:* Complex drawings and images might not translate well to, for example, a newsletter or on a business card. So keep your logo as clean and simple as possible.

Clean. Simple. To the point. . . . That's what you're going for.

Construct an Elevator Pitch

This is not to be confused with your slogan. It's something a little longer, but still very tight.

Imagine you happen to grab the same elevator as the CEO whose attention you've been trying to get for months. Now, you have him cornered. You're both going to the thirty-second floor, and you have about ten seconds flat to tell him what you do and how you can benefit his firm.

This is your elevator speech, and it should become second nature to you for networking purposes.

It should not only answer the question, "What do you do?" but it should be framed in a way to make the listener curious enough to want to know more. This is why a benefit should be a part of it. Remember, all human beings are driven by the WIIFM factor.

Here's a great example of an elevator speech from the site Improv Andy.com. It's for a Business Coach.

When was the last time you printed out and saved a thank-you e-mail? I was at a trade show recently and took digital pictures of the booths of my prospects. When I got back to the office I sent each one a thank-you card with a picture of their booth on it. When I stopped by for a sales call a few weeks later, the card was proudly displayed on their desk.

When you're ready to make a lasting impression, hand me your business card for a free walk-through of our proprietary system. My name is _____ and I want you to build better business relationships through effective follow-up.

There are tons of these pitches on this site. This one stood out because it tells a story, defines concrete results, showcases a unique approach, and is not "salesy" at all.

What could you say to prospects to get across what you do, in an interesting way, that piques their interest and illustrates how they can benefit?

Touch on these elements, and you just may have a winner.

You'll fine-tune your elevator speech over time, so don't worry about it being letter perfect. But do practice it. Say it out loud. Test it on friends and family. If you find that it's not flowing naturally, that's a clue that maybe you need to change the wording. Remember, it should flow, it shouldn't sound like a sales pitch, and the main goal is to arouse the interest of prospects to make them want to learn more.

Conclusion

Entire college courses, books, and degrees cover branding. And there's always something new coming down the pike to learn. But these are the foundational building blocks you need to get started.

Many freelancers never get around to even thinking about branding their business. So you're already leagues ahead by doing the basics outlined here.

Chapter 6

Marketing 101

Marketing is the lifeblood of every enterprise—small or large, free-lance or traditional business—simply because until a sale happens no other systems you put in place will be used. There will be:

- No invoices generated
- No payments to process
- No outside contractors hired

Marketing consists of getting a mutually beneficial exchange to take place between a buyer (your potential client) and a seller (you, the freelancer). Then, all the processes and procedures you've set up are triggered into action. This is why it's important to understand what goes into a successful marketing plan, which is what is discussed in this chapter, beginning with one of the biggest questions many freelancers have: Should you specialize, or not?

To Niche or Not to Niche

A creative director at a pharmaceutical ad agency needs a freelance copywriter to write a brochure explaining the benefits of a new drug that's coming to market. He places an ad. Tons of responses start coming in from freelance copywriters.

Who do you think has a better chance of landing the job: a freelance writer with tons of experience in many different niches, who may have amazing writing samples, or a copywriter who specializes in medical content?

The freelance medical copywriter, right? She'll write copy that finds its audience because she's an expert in communicating with that audience. So the question is not if you should niche, but how to define your niche. Once you define it, it will be much easier to craft a marketing message that resonates.

The Five Ws of Marketing

Who? What? Where? When? Why? Answering these questions will make it pretty easy to zero in on your target market.

Who Is Your Target Market?

The most effective way to answer this question is to research the demographics and psychographics of your targeted niche. In case you're wondering what demographics and psychographics are, these are terms advertising professionals use to refer to what I call "hard" and "soft" variables of your target marketing. Psychographics encompasses soft variables such as personality, values, attitudes, interests, and lifestyle. Demographics are the hard variables that can be readily measured, such as age, gender, and race.

Think about your ideal prospect as if he were sitting across the table from you. Now, picture specifics like:

- What is he wearing?
- Who are his friends?
- Where did he go to school?
- What kind of job does he have?

- What is his marital status?
- How often does he go out?
- What kind of restaurants does he frequent?
- What does he like to do on the weekend?
- What kind of music does he like to listen to, what books does he like to read, what movies has he probably seen?

By doing this type of visualization, you bring your ideal customer alive. He becomes a real creature of your imagination, and you can devise a marketing message to suit him.

What Are Your Target Market's Pain Points?

A pain point, in business speak, is a problem to which your ideal customer wants a solution. There are several ways to find these out. You can:

- Scour industry-specific forums.
- Use social media. For example, join targeted groups on popular sites such as LinkedIn and Facebook. You'd be amazed at just how much information, including gripes, people share in these forums.
- Join professional trade organizations pertinent to a defined niche.
- Attend conferences and seminars—many of which you can find for free, especially online webinars.

One of the best ways to find out the pain points of a targeted audience is to go directly to the source. After becoming a trusted, professional colleague, many industry insiders will have no problem sharing this type of information with you. This is one reason it's important to build relationships in any niche you're thinking of targeting. Some other reasons are: It keeps you abreast of what's going on in the industry; it requires less hard selling over time; and it leads to referrals and repeat clients because it nurtures a pipeline of relationships you can depend on.

Where Do They Hang Out?

You want to know where they congregate online and offline. Find this out via industry associations, online discussion groups and forums, niche blogs, and so on.

FREELANCER TIP

Did you know that each social media outlet has defined demographics? They do. According to Pew Research Center, women dominate Pinterest; 44 percent of them used the site, as opposed to just 16 percent of men. They tend to be fifty or younger (37 percent); just 22 percent are over fifty.

LinkedIn is the only major social media platform for which usage rates are higher among 30- to 49-year-olds than among 18- to 29-year-olds. Fully 46% of online adults who have graduated from college are LinkedIn users, compared with just 9% of online adults with a high school diploma or less.

You can have the best marketing message and product or service out there, but if you're not reaching your intended market, it won't mean diddly-squat.

When Do They Need Your Services?

One simple way to find this out is to ask. Create a questionnaire to distribute. It can be done via mail or e-mail. Keep it short and simple in order to encourage as many responses as possible.

Another way is to keep a running poll on your website with a few questions you'd like answers to. Via free polling software available online, such as MicroPoll and EasyPolls, you can have a poll up and going on your website in minutes.

Why Do They Need Your Services?

What are you offering them that they can't get anywhere else? This will be discussed more in the next section on determining your unique selling point (USP).

Key Questions to Consider

Once you've defined your target market, you need to further refine your understanding of it. To that end, here are some questions you should ask yourself:

1. Is the niche broad enough to support your business goals? You must have enough potential customers to run a sustainable freelance business.
2. Is the market fragmented, or relatively easy to reach? This can be a good or a bad thing. Even if there are enough customers to market to, if they're too hard to reach, it can cost you big in time and resources. On the plus side, there may be a sub-niche you hadn't even thought of that is easy to reach that you can target instead.
3. Can they afford your rates?
4. Will they see a need for what you're offering?

What a USP Is and Why You Need One

Part of successfully marketing and selling your freelancing to a niche market is determining what makes you unique. This is where the USP, first mentioned in Chapter 3, comes in.

To refresh your memory, as defined in Chapter 3, a USP is the element that makes your product or service different from that of competitors. Think of it as what you have, offer, or do that your competitors don't.

It's the soul of a business because it takes some soul-searching to define clearly. It will be the foundation of your marketing and branding efforts, and if it's well thought out, it will eliminate competitors instead of pitting you against them.

The most important thing to remember about a USP is that it should center on a benefit to the customer.

The Four Ps of the Marketing Mix

The USP helps businesses define their product or brand. It's often associated with the following four Ps of marketing: product, price, promotion, and placement.

1. Product

This can be either a tangible good or a service.

How can you use your product to develop a USP? What's unique about your product? What differentiates it from others? What do consumers, want, need, or expect when they purchase it? Remember, it's almost never about the product itself. Your client is always buying a benefit (it makes them feel younger; it frees up more time to spend with their family; it offers them financial freedom; etc.).

2. Price

This is how much you decide to sell your product for.

How can you use price to develop a USP? What is the perceived value of your product? If you're the cheapest, don't be afraid to say so. If you're the most expensive, don't shy away from that either. You can build your brand around value and exclusivity—you don't necessarily have to underprice the competition.

3. Promotion

Promotion is how you market your product—everything from social media, to e-mail, to seminars, and personal consultations.

How can you use promotion to develop a USP? When you're marketing your product, how can you disseminate relevant information that differentiates you from others? Remember: benefit, benefit, benefit. What's in it for the customer?

4. Placement

This is where you place your product so that customers can find you. It's positioning your product in ideal locations so prospects can find you, and you can convert them into actual paying customers.

How can you use placement to develop a USP? Based on your niche, what is the most effective way to get your product into your customers' hands?

As you can see, your USP can be found in any or all of the four Ps.

How to Develop Your USP

Now that you know what a USP is and why you need one, here's how to go about developing one.

Research the Competition

You did this when you did your market analysis. It's a good place to start because you probably won't have any data (or very little) about your own freelancing business. So spy on your competition.

Determine what their USPs are—even if they haven't spelled them out in a slogan. You're going to be amazed at just how many don't have one, which gives you a leg up, by the way. Research five to ten freelance businesses in your niche. Ask yourself how your business is different. What can you do to stand out from them and make customers want to patronize you instead? Remember, focus on client benefits.

What are your competitors doing that's working, that you can improve on and/or put a different twist on? Or, what are they not doing that you could do?

Know Your Customer

The more you know about your target customers and their lives, the easier it will be for you to sell to them. So get to know your market intimately. That's why we started your business plan with the market analysis and why you were asked to clearly define your target market.

Analyze Your Business

This requires stepping back from your business and putting yourself in your customers' shoes. The reason it's important to do this is, you're likely too close to your freelance business to be objective. So flip the script, so to speak.

Look objectively at your business and with your ideal customer in mind, ask, "What do they really want? Does what I offer suit their needs?" And please remember—this can't be repeated enough—it's never just about your product or service. It's the benefit it provides the customer. For example, when a woman buys perfume, she's not buying a scent; she's buying how that scent makes her feel and how it makes her appear to others. It could be that it reminds her of the night her husband proposed, or the way her mother smelled, or that it makes her feel sexy.

If you're a web designer and a new restaurant owner hires you to design her website, she's not hiring you for your web design skills. She's hiring you to make her dream of being a successful restaurateur come alive, to have customers beating down her door, to get noticed so that all-important restaurant critic comes to eat, gives her a fabulous review, and makes her the next Julia Child.

This is what she's really paying you for. Is your business selling this?

Solicit Feedback

Where possible, solicit feedback from your target market. Again, this can be done vicariously through your competition. Thanks to blogs and other online outlets these days, it's relatively easy to gain insight into the pain points of a defined market and how they are, or are not, being addressed.

You can also go to your local SBA and ask a member of SCORE to help you. (See Chapter 1.)

Invite friends and family over for a potluck and ask them to act as an impromptu focus group. Let them know you want them to be brutally honest.

You could always, of course, hire a marketing firm to help you. This might cost a pretty penny, but if you can afford it, then go for it. Just be sure to ask for referrals upfront and do check them out.

Once you've settled on your USP, make sure to market the heck out of it. Make it part of your marketing arsenal. It should be everywhere—your website, your social media accounts, your brochures, in your news-letters, and so on. Remember, you're building a brand. Before you know it, your customers will start to rely on you for it—and you'll realize that your message is not only getting through, it's sticking.

Competition: What You Need to Know

All businesses face competition, especially in today's global economy where you compete not only with Joe Schmoe down the street, but Jane Doe in Australia and Xian Lee in China and José Gonzalez in Mexico and . . . you get the picture.

Freelancing can be a very insular profession, one where it's easy to tune out everything but the project(s) currently before you. This can be dangerous, though, because you run the risk of tuning out your competition. You can't afford to do this because they can save you a lot of time and money.

When you first start, use your competition to guide you in making important decisions such as:

- How to set your prices
- What products and services to offer

- The most effective way to ship/deliver
- How to reach your market
- What technology to use to make your business more efficient

Look at their websites, blogs, newsletters, annual reports, marketing materials, leading industry professionals, and networking organizations to find out what they're up to and how it can benefit you.

Use Competitor Information to Your Advantage

Once you gather information, you can use it to do some of the following:

- *Take the lead.* Have you been hearing rumblings that customers want something different but nobody has taken the initiative to offer it? That could be you. Be an innovator! If everybody is doing the same thing, forge a new path, especially when research tells you that there's an unfulfilled need there.
- *Attack.* Exploit their weakness(es). If you position your company to fulfill a need that is a glaring flaw for competitors, your business will be hard to ignore. Remember, play nice. Never directly attack a business. Let the way you serve your customers do all the "talking."
- *Partner.* One of the best ways to start getting business, especially when you're just starting out, is to seek overflow from existing businesses. This is an often-overlooked way to step into the marketplace as a new freelancer. You can also lower expenses, by doing some co-op advertising, for example.

Don't assume that just because a business is a competitor that they're your enemy. Nothing could be further from the truth. As the information here highlights, they are in fact one of your greatest allies.

Your competitors are a veritable treasure trove of information. When you're first starting out, you're going to have a lot on your plate. There's no need to reinvent the wheel. As many of your competitors have already done a lot of the heavy lifting in terms of market research, all you have to do is leverage it to your advantage.

Free or Low-Cost Marketing That Works

The wonderful thing about the Internet is that you don't have to spend any money to make money these days. In fact, free marketing can be just as, or even more, effective than paid advertising. Following are two often underused methods.

Content Marketing

If you haven't heard this phrase yet, don't get overwhelmed with it as you delve into marketing avenues for your freelance business. Once you understand the basics, it isn't as complicated as it might sound. What is it? According to the Content Marketing Institute (CMI):

Content marketing is a strategic marketing approach focused on creating and distributing valuable, relevant, and consistent content to attract and retain a clearly defined audience—and, ultimately, to drive profitable customer action.

When people go online, they go online to search for information to help them make a decision.

Understanding how people search for that information is the next step. Google's data analysis website (www.ThinkwithGoogle .com) provides the following statistics on business-to-business (B2B) searches:

- 71% of B2B researchers start their research with a generic search.
- Research shows that those involved in the B2B buying process are already 57% of the way down the path to a decision before they'll actually perform an action on your site.

- 90% of B2B researchers who are online use search specifically to research business purchases.

These stats underscore why content marketing is so important. Prospects don't want to be sold to these days. They're smart. They already know you want to make a sale.

FREELANCER TIP

How often should you market with content? It all depends on you, your industry, your budget, and so forth. If your business is online personal training, you may be in touch every day with a diet tip or a ten-minute workout. If you own a resume-writing service, you may be in touch once a month, offering job-finding tips in a sluggish economy.

At a bare minimum no matter what type of freelance business you start, you should reach out to prospects at least once a month. Once-a-week contact is better.

What they want is to be educated about your product so that they can make the most informed decision possible. Following are some content marketing areas that can help you turn prospects into paying customers:

- Blogging
- Newsletters
- White papers
- Case studies (For example, if you've had a client you've helped overcome a specific pain point that is common to a certain niche, then you can make a case study out of it and post it to your website as a free download of how you can help prospects overcome their problem.)

- SlideShares
- Video (yes, this is content!)
- Infographics
- Memes
- eBooks
- Special reports
- Interviews
- Tutorials
- Product reviews
- Editorials

You get the idea, right?

FREELANCER TIP

Special reports are similar to case studies in that they're a teaching tool to help prospects understand how you can help them. For example, I wrote a special report for my business when I first started out as an SEO writer. Many of the prospects I was targeting didn't even know what "SEO" was. They knew that they wanted their website to be pulling in more sales and leads, but they didn't know how to go about it. As an SEO writer, I wrote up a special report explaining how SEO content was integral to helping a website deliver sales and leads. I uploaded it as a PDF file to my website; it was a free download. It explained what SEO writing was and how it could help a prospect get more sales and leads from their sites. I got a lot of business for years from this one report. This is the power of special reports.

Cost of Content Marketing

Content marketing will cost you about $10 per month using list management software such as AWeber, GetResponse, and

MailChimp. As your subscriber list grows, so will your costs, but usually this doesn't happen until you have 1,000–2,500 or more subscribers.

Cold-Calling

Most freelancers hate to do it, but the fact is, cold-calling works. Perhaps the reason is, many never screw up the courage to pick up the phone; hence, for the few who do, there's less competition when this type of marketing is used.

One aspect of cold-calling that makes it scary is that you don't know what to say. And, oh yeah, there is that fear of rejection. Remember in Chapter 1 when we talked about how to overcome fear of rejection? Use those same techniques to overcome your fear of cold-calling.

Now let's discuss some concrete things you can do to make cold-calling less scary.

1. Mentally prepare. Acknowledge your fear. Put it out there, take a deep breath, and vow to move forward. It does get easier.
2. Target your audience. Only cold-call your ideal client as identified in your market research. This way, you don't waste time and nervous energy calling on the wrong people. The more targeted your calls are, the more quickly you get to a yes. And there's nothing like a yes to make you excited enough to make that next call.
3. Reach out and touch. Before you call, send an e-mail, a postcard, a sales letter—something to make the call a warm one. This gives you a jumping-off point for the conversation: "This is Mary Jackson from Jackson Accounting Services. I sent you that industry report last week and told you I'd be following up this week. . . ." See how much more comfortable that can be than just a regular cold call?
4. Create a short script. Knowing what you will say before you pick up the phone will go a long way toward making it less

scary. A written script will help keep you focused on the points you want to make. All you need are a few short sentences that give the prospect a description of your services and a compelling reason to give you a shot (state a benefit). Do your research beforehand and come up with possible objections so you can counter with specific details, statistics, and research.

5. Practice. The only way to get comfortable making cold calls is to practice. Force yourself to make a certain number each day. Do them first thing in the morning so you don't procrastinate and talk yourself out of ever getting around to it.

There's a reason this time-honored method of marketing has been around for so long. It works. The key to success with it is to stay targeted in your message and focused only on those who are already primed and ready to buy what you have to offer.

Cost of Cold-Calling

The best part of this form of marketing? It can be free or low-cost for the most part, especially if you're not calling internationally and use technology like Voice over Internet Protocol (VoIP), which enables you to make and receive calls through the Internet instead of a traditional phone carrier. Most VoIP service carriers offer unlimited U.S. calls and reasonably priced international calls, which helps you keep your phone bill in check.

Your Website

We live in a wired world in a global economy. You cannot afford not to have a website. The good news is, it's so easy to get one these days that a twelve-year-old can do it.

A basic website is all you need to get started. If you don't know how to update it yourself and you don't have a lot of money, this is something you're going to need to learn how to do pronto. Why?

Because it can cost you a fortune if you have to pay someone every time you want to change a price, or add a sample, or announce an upcoming seminar or sale.

Websites these days are designed, for the most part, in WordPress, an online, open-source website creation tool. In non-geek speak, it's known as a content management system (CMS).

Almost a quarter of all the websites and blogs online today are powered by this powerful content management system. So if you're getting a website, most likely, you'll be getting one that's designed using WordPress.

Once you learn how, it's very easy to add a post, upload video, or insert graphics. Even if you don't have a lot of money, investing in a basic web design class should be one of the first expenses you undertake as a freelancer.

Free versus Paid Web Hosting

There are many free website options that you don't have to pay hosting fees for, e.g., Blogger, Weebly, and Wix. Stay away from them. You always want to register your own domain name and pay for your own web hosting.

This is your business and with websites being so cheap, there's no excuse not to register your own domain name and pay for hosting. Once you pay for a domain name—which can cost less than $5 or $10, web hosting can be less than $10 per month.

Also, if you decide to get one of those free websites, you run the risk of violating terms of service agreements. Many of the free sites come with stringent terms of service that dictate what can and can't be said or offered on it. You could be violating some terms of service you don't even know about. You'll log onto your site one day and find a notice like: "This site violates our Terms of Service. It has been removed." Poof! Your site is gone, along with all your carefully crafted content, graphics, and videos.

You may also lose clients. Are you really worth what you're charging if you can't even afford to invest $10 a month to have a professionally hosted site? This is the thought that may run through a prospect's mind.

Finally, free websites tend to look unprofessional. Your website is your business face to the world. Everybody knows ABCsite.blogspot .com is a free site, as opposed to yourbusiness.com. Now that's a professional domain name.

Your website is another facet of your business's brand. It speaks to what goes on in a prospect's mind when he views it. Every facet of your business sends a message about it, how it operates, and what its core values and beliefs are.

A free site—no matter how well designed—will be in conflict with that message because it says to prospective clients loud and clear, I don't care enough to invest in my business this way. Yet, you expect them to believe that you'll make a major investment in their business, in their project.

While many freelancers have free websites, there's no way to judge how much business you lose because of something you don't do. So don't run the risk of tarnishing your reputation for something that is such a minor investment.

Do You Need a Website or a Blog?

A blog and a website are both websites, but blogs have interactive components that most websites don't. Conversely, websites tend to be more of a portfolio, an online company brochure.

What purpose will your web presence serve? Once you know what you want your web presence to do for you, it will be easy to decide if it should be a blog or a website. For example, if you're going to start a newsletter to attract subscribers so you can grow your list, then you definitely want a blog because every post you add is a new page. With a website, when you add a new page, you add it independently of other pages on the site. So if, for example, you forget to put the subscribe button on that page, it won't show up.

With a blog, all pages automatically look the same. You don't have to remember to add individual features such as the subscriber buttons, date, blog, or links to the other pages on your site. All of this is done for you.

This is why it's prudent to get a blog instead of a website these days. Even if you just use it as a static web presence, if you do decide to start blogging, you won't have to have your site redesigned or reinstalled. So just get a blog from the beginning.

Now let's turn to how to get one, and what to put on it.

FREELANCER TIP

The words *blog* and *website* are often used interchangeably, herein, and on the web in general.

DIY Option

Web design doesn't have to cost a fortune. Most web hosting companies have do-it-yourself (DIY) options that come complete with sleek templates that you can just drag and drop graphics and content into—and bam!—you have a website overnight.

It really is that simple. Here are some of the leading web hosting companies in 2016:

- eHost.com
- iPage.com
- Web.com
- Bluehost.com
- JustHost.com
- IdeaHost.com
- InMotionHosting.com
- HostGator.com
- HostPapa.com
- GoDaddy.com

Visit any of these sites and look for wording like "website builder." Poke around. You'll find thousands (yes, thousands!) of gorgeous, predesigned templates, straightforward instructions, and access to help centers to get you started.

And the cost—it's nominal for simple sites, which is all most free-lancers need just starting out. For less than $10 per month, you can have a professional-looking site that gives prospects all the information they need to start doing business with you.

FREELANCER TIP

Here are some tips for choosing a web designer. Conduct online research on them/their firm.

- Look at their portfolios.
- Ask for and check references.
- Assess their professionalism: For example, how much time did they spend upfront asking you questions to clarify what you want? Do they have some type of intake questionnaire?
- How do they charge (is it by the hour, by the project)?
- What kind of back-end support do they offer?
- How long have they been in business?
- Will you own the copyright to any logos or graphics they create for you, or does this cost extra?
- Do you own the final design of the site and will have control over it, or will they?

Paid Option

If you don't want to go the DIY route, you can always hire a web designer to build one for you. Costs can range anywhere from a few dollars to a few thousand dollars. It all depends on what you want and need and whom you hire.

Web design is like the Wild West. Prices are all over the place. You can find a quality designer on freelance sites such as Upwork or on free classified ad sites such as Craigslist, or you can go with a referral from a friend. The guy from Craigslist may charge you $200, while a firm on Upwork may quote you $2,000 for the same design. The key is to research, research, research.

The Most Important Thing to Remember

If you know nothing about design, bone up on it before you hire a designer. The most important things you're going to want the answers to are who owns the copyright and who owns the future design of the site. You want all work done by your web designer under a work-for-hire agreement, with all rights wholly belonging and reverting to you upon completion. This includes access to your website. Be sure to get this in writing.

Trust your gut. If for any reason something in your gut says no about the way a particular designer or firm treats you, keep looking. There are many web designers to choose from. There's no reason to hire one you don't wholly trust right from the beginning.

What to Put on Your Website

This can be different for every freelancer, but a basic freelance site should include the following pages.

- *Services*: A list of all the services you offer. If you offer many, you might want to break them down into separate pages. But if you just have a few, you can put them all on one page.
- *About*: Many might not think of this as a necessary page, but it is because it's that handshake, that smile, and that direct eye contact you don't get to give in person. People do business with people they know, like, and trust. Your about page introduces prospects to you—the person behind the business. Be sure to include a professional, appropriate photo.

- *Contact info*: List all the ways you can be contacted: e-mail, cell, Skype, social media, etc.
- *Work samples*: Anything that showcases what you've done—even if it's a sample you create just for your site and not an actual client. Prospective clients need something to assess. Give it to them.
- *Opt-in option*: You should always have a way to capture visitor information (e.g., subscribe to our newsletter), even if you have no plans to use it in the immediate future.

You've done the hard part of getting a prospect to land on your website. Don't let him leave without asking for a way to keep in contact with him. You never know where your next job is going to come from.

Having a home-grown subscriber list that you keep in contact with regularly—even just sending out a joke of the day or a link weekly to the most important happenings in your industry—is a way to stay in the customer's mind. So start building this list from day one. It's not optional; it's necessary.

These are the five necessary pages of your website. Some others you might want to include are:

- *Testimonials*: Written proof from past clients about how wonderfully you serviced them goes a long way toward getting future jobs. It builds your brand and instills customer trust. Try to cultivate testimonials from clients who give you permission to use their full names, titles, and the companies they represent.
- *Rates/prices*: Some freelancers list their rates; others don't. It's a personal choice. If you're torn about whether or not to list rates, look to your competition. Do most of them list their rates, or not?
- *Client questionnaire*: You don't want to scare prospects away by giving them too much upfront work to do, but a client questionnaire can go a long way toward prequalifying prospects for

you. If you decide to put one up, make it short and sweet, asking only the info you absolutely, positively must have in order to help you decide if a prospect is a good fit. You might want to wait to add this to your site until you're a bit more established and have the luxury of qualifying prospects in this manner; otherwise you run the risk of scaring off a client before you ever get to "meet" them.

Make Sure Your Site Is Mobile Ready

Whether you create a static website or an interactive blog, make sure it's mobile ready because that's how customers are accessing the web these days. In fact, many are no longer using their computers and laptops to access the web, but rather are doing so only via mobile devices. Proof? An article on comScore, "2015 U.S. Digital Future in Focus," says:

More than 75 percent of all Americans who use the Internet (age 18+) now access digital content on both desktop and mobile devices, which is an increase from 68 percent from a year ago. Mobile-only Internet usage is also becoming more common, driven predominantly by millennials, of which 21 percent are *no longer using desktop computers* [emphasis added] to go online.

Meanwhile, the 55-years-and-older consumer segment is actually the fastest growing faction of mobile users, increasing its combined multi-platform and mobile-only share of audience from 60 percent to 74 percent in the past year.

Other factors to consider:

- *Make sure it loads fast.* Mobile users are an impatient lot. Studies have shown that almost 60 percent will abandon a site if it takes more than three seconds to load.
- *Make buttons easy to find.* If they're ready to take action, they want to be able to easily find the buttons they need to do so.

So make sure your call-to-action buttons (e.g., order, subscribe, call) are easy to find.

- *Give it a clean design.* While customers want to be able to find the buttons to take actions, they don't want the design to be so sloppy that they keep accidentally hitting buttons they don't want to hit. So make sure your design is clean and well thought out. User engagement should be designed for touch screens for ease of swiping, scrolling, and tapping. Also keep in mind that as the screen is small, users don't want to have to swipe, scroll, or tap a gazillion times to complete an action. Keep it simple.
- *Compress graphics.* This makes your site load faster.

Chapter 7

How to Land Your First Client(s)

Landing clients—especially those first few—can seem like climbing Mount Everest. First, you don't know what to do. Then, when you figure out what to do, you doubt that you're doing it right. Then, after you've reached the depths of your self-confidence and forged ahead anyway, you may feel sick from putting yourself out there.

It's all normal. It really is. This is why you have to flip the mental switch in your mind and think of it as, "How can I help X business?" instead of "How can I land that gig?"

The following sections detail three ways to land those precious first few clients. Once you do, your confidence will grow—and you'll wonder what was so scary in the first place.

1. Join a Chamber of Commerce

Every freelancer should join a chamber of commerce because it's where the business leaders in a given community are. Talk about reaching a decision-maker—they're right there in front of you, scoffing down free doughnuts and coffee!

Here are three more good reasons to join:

1. You get seamless leads and referrals.
2. There's less competition.
3. It builds trust.

Let's explore each one of these.

Get Leads and Referrals

The definition of a chamber of commerce is "a local association to promote and protect the interests of the business community in a particular place."

Notice the "to promote" part? Most chambers have a dedicated leads/referrals/networking component to them. It's the reason most small businesses in a community join. This can help you land business fast. How? Why?

Consider this—people do business with those they know, like, and trust. A chamber provides you the format to cultivate all three of these.

Know

When you join a chamber, you'll be called upon to introduce yourself to the existing members. Usually, everyone is sitting around a table. Once the meeting commences, one of the first things members do is ask new and/or guest members to introduce themselves. So you may stand and say the following:

I'm Sue from Sue's Web Design. I just relocated here from Flint, Michigan, where the winters are brutally cold. My mother is getting older and as I can essentially work from anywhere, I thought, why not join her here in sunny Miami. I haven't regretted the decision.

Then, everyone will welcome you, and they'll move on to the next new and/or visiting guest. So, now people know who you are.

Say you decide to join and you attend every week faithfully. Most chambers meet weekly at a minimum; some meet several times a week. You become friends with Stanley, who owns a popular local printing shop. You tend to gravitate to each other over coffee before the beginning of each meeting. You also regularly make small talk with several other members, a couple of whom you've run into around town.

Like

Stanley says to Mary, another chamber member, "Wow, that Sue, she sure is nice."

"Yes," she is, Mary agrees. "In fact, I thought of her the other day. A Realtor friend of mine was telling me that she needs a completely new website. Her nephew did her old one, but he just went off to college and she has no clue about web design."

Trust

"I've seen some of her work," Stanley says. "I asked her opinion on a few logos I came up with for one of my restaurant customers, and I took her suggestions. My client has never been so happy.

"I asked her to show me her portfolio, and boy, she's good. In my opinion, you can't go wrong at least talking to her about it. I'm not sure what her rates are, but she'll give you some good ideas for your redesign. She sure helped me out—and she didn't charge me a dime, even though I offered to pay her a consultation fee."

"Thanks for the referral, Stan. I'll do that," Mary says.

That's how easy it can be to land jobs when you belong to a chamber of commerce and regularly attend meetings. It's all about building relationships. Once that is in place, you can gain lifelong clients who wouldn't dream of using someone else—even when that someone else is cheaper—because they know, like, and trust you.

There's another factor at work here—complacency. Most people have a referral network in place, and they rarely change it unless something goes wrong. It's just human nature to continue to do what works unless some force propels you to do something different.

Human beings are creatures of habit. If you become a part of someone's referral network, she'll refer you over and over again. Of course, you do the same for them.

This is why it's such a good idea to join a chamber. It can't be beat for making connections with the business leaders in your community and becoming a part of their referral network.

Lessen the Competition

Every business has competition, but you lessen that competition when you join a chamber because of the reasons listed in the previous section.

Who do you think is more likely to give you business? Someone you network with on a regular basis, or someone you happen to cold-call or send an e-mail to? The person who sees you week in and week out, right?

Many freelancers never think to join a chamber because they think of it as a fuddy-duddy organization for "other" professionals in their community—doctors, lawyers, and insurance salesmen. For sure, those people are there.

But these professionals also need web design services, copywriting services, accounting and billing services, marketing, and PR services—in short, whatever services you offer, there's a business that needs it. Many of them can be found right in your chamber. The best part? Because you're likely to be one of the only freelancers in your chamber who offers a particular service, you lessen the competition significantly.

Build Trust

Many chambers have seals that you can include in your marketing materials that say something to the effect of, "Proud member of the (City Name) Chamber of Commerce."

Using that seal on your PR material is a seamless way to instill trust in your customers because first, people automatically infer that your business must be legitimate if it belongs to a business chamber, and second, it gives them an easy way to investigate your business if they want to. If you've been a part of a chamber for a while, you're likely to get good recommendations from other business owners who belong to it—even if you haven't worked with them directly.

Now that you know why it's a good idea to join an organization such as this when you first start out as a freelancer, here's what to look for before joining.

What to Look for in a Chamber

If your local chamber doesn't offer the following, look for one in the largest city closest to you that does. A chamber of commerce is only as good as the business owners who participate in it, and not all chambers are equal.

Regular meetings: Depending on how large or small a chamber is, it may have a couple of meetings a week, or a couple per day. Most offer at least two per week—one in the morning and one in the evening.

The rationale is, there are early birds and night owls—so if you can't make a morning meeting, then you can catch one in the late afternoon or evening. Many small and micro-business owners still work full- or part-time jobs, so chambers meetings held at different times can accommodate these varying schedules.

As a general rule, afternoon meetings tend to be more heavily attended than early morning or evening ones. But attend all of them initially—schedule permitting—to see which ones work best for you.

Dedicated lead sessions: These are sessions specifically designed for members to network and actively match businesses seeking certain products and services to those that offer them. Here's a common way many of these networking sessions are structured:

Usually, there's a fifteen- or twenty-minute mingling session that allows members to get coffee, chat, and get to know one another. Thereafter, the meeting is officially called to order.

Once everyone is seated, the chamber member in charge will go around the table, giving members a chance to do a thirty-second or so spiel about their business. You can think of this as an expanded "elevator speech" or mini-commercial for your business in which you explain what you do. The most important part of this speech is, "What's a good lead for you *today*?"

Many members forget to focus on this part. The reason it's important is, if you've been going to meetings for a while, everyone will more or less know what you do, but a lead session gives you a chance to get specific about what type of client you're looking for at the moment.

For example, if you're a freelance recruiter/headhunter and you've just met this extremely talented legal secretary who specializes in patent law, you might say:

> "I'm Sue from Sue's Legal Recruiting. We staff all kinds of legal positions—from court reporters to paralegals. However, a good lead for me today is a firm who is seeking a legal secretary with patent law experience. I've just interviewed a multi-talented candidate who just relocated and is seeking a position."

See how this is different from a general spiel about your business? Someone just might know someone (or be that someone) who is looking for specialized talent like this. Another more general—yet specific—pitch might go something like this:

> "I'm Robert Land, head of Land's Online Marketing Services. We provide a wide range of services that help you get found—online and off. What I've noticed is that many companies haven't taken advantage of mixed media online. They blog and use newsletters, for example, but don't have any videos on their site. This is missing out on a huge amount of YouTube traffic.
>
> "And just in case you're wondering just how much traffic that is, did you know that YouTube has over a billion users worldwide? That's almost a third of all people who are online. Imagine! One out of every three people who logs on is on YouTube. And get this—you can navigate YouTube in seventy-six different

languages. This covers 95 percent of the entire population who are online. So it's a huge—huge!—traffic source. But, if you don't have video on your site, you're missing out on all of it. Ready to change that?

"We have an introductory video marketing package to get those who aren't leveraging this monstrous online marketing source. That's a good lead for me today—anyone who's ready to start increasing sales, just by putting some easy-to-get videos on their site. We can have some videos on your site within a couple of days—really. I'll be around for a while after the meeting to answer any specifics. Thank you."

Again, the pitch is specific to this freelancer's video marketing services, even though he offers a wide range of online marketing services. This is why lead meetings can be so fruitful—you're right there in the room with people who may need your services (or know of others who do)—telling them exactly what you can do for them *today*. You just can't get more effective marketing than this.

During the meeting, some type of lead form or networking slip is used. These allow you to fill in the info of a presenter you hear who may be a good lead for you or someone you know. For example, take Sue the recruiter who has a legal secretary she's trying to place.

Stan may have a friend who works for a major law firm. He doesn't know if it's patent or not, but he may write down Sue's information, along with his friend's information. At the end of the lead session, he'll hand the slip to Sue, saying something like, "I don't know what kind of law they practice, but my friend Bob works at a law firm downtown and I was at his place for a barbecue last week and I remember him saying something about them needing some help. Here's his info. Tell him I gave it to you. Hope it works out."

Even if Bob turns out to specialize in criminal law, he may know of a friend who works in patent law who could use Sue's candidate.

This is classic networking. It all starts with joining a chamber, and getting them to know who you are and the services you provide.

Not to beat a dead horse, but a chamber membership is only as good as your participation level. So don't join and be a ghost. Join—and go!

Cost to Join a Chamber

Most chambers of commerce have tiered levels of pricing, usually based on business size. They can range from a few hundred bucks per year, on up to $10,000 or more.

The more expensive memberships are usually bought by the big businesses in a community. As a freelancer, a basic membership is all you'll need—one that gives you the right to participate in things like lead sessions.

If you can afford it, this is one of the first things you should do when you decide to freelance. One job from a chamber member can not only pay your membership dues for an entire year (based on your rates, of course), but it opens the doors to the business movers and shakers in your community.

2. Get Your Former Employer on Board

This way of landing clients is obvious, but can be severely overlooked by aspiring freelancers. It's because many aren't quite sure how to go about it—at least not in a strategic manner.

> *"Don't burn bridges. You'll be surprised how many times you have to cross the same river."*
> —H. JACKSON BROWN JR., INSPIRATIONAL AUTHOR

In today's digital society, this has never been more important. For example, when you log onto LinkedIn, how do you start "linking up" with people? By those you already know, right? And this usually consists of former coworkers.

As you can glean from the previous networking examples, burning a bridge today can be akin to business suicide because it spreads like wildfire. Unless you live off the grid, it's practically impossible to disappear. So keep your links alive, well, and strong, for they can be an amazing resource to jump-start your freelance career.

In fact, following is a four-step plan for turning your former employer into one of your first clients.

Turning Your Employer Into Your Freelance Client

You have an in-built advantage with your current employer, which, if leveraged correctly, can give you your first job as you embark on this exciting new journey. Here's how to increase your chance of leaving your job with a firm offer of work in hand from your employer.

Plan Your Exit

It's wise to start planning your exit strategy six months to a year out. Can you do it in less time? Sure, but like almost anything in life, the more time you put into the planning phase, the more you increase your chances of success.

Give Proof of Work

Of course, your current employer already knows what you're capable of. But in corporate America, positions tend to be more segmented than when you freelance. What does this mean and why is it important?

What it means is, when you work full-time, you usually have a job description that explains what your duties and responsibilities are. You complete your part, then hand it off to another department to complete their part, and so on and so on until the job is done.

When you freelance, more than likely there will be no other departments to send jobs off to once your portion is complete. You're usually responsible for a job from beginning to end. If that means learning a new skill, you do it. If that means farming out part of the project to another freelancer, you do it.

Being responsible for a project from beginning to end helps you build a portfolio that showcases a range of work over and beyond what you may be responsible for in a full-time job. It builds other skill sets as well, for example: sourcing and hiring talent; invoicing and paying outside vendors; and strategizing a project from conception to completion, to name a few.

This is why so many freelancers tend to have such diverse skill sets. What they don't know, they have to learn—which can expand their skill sets much faster than their nine-to-five counterparts. An article on the Crunch blog explains:

> Freelancers are 35% more likely than firms to combine diverse skills and knowledge sets in their work, according to a recent report from research and development project, Brighton Fuse. The report established three categories—unfused, fused, and superfused—to determine the level of skills diversity.
>
> The findings showed that 46.7% of freelancers were superfused, in that combining skill sets was integral to their work. In comparison, only 34.7% of firms identified as being "superfused." Freelancers earned more money depending on the diversity of their skills, with "superfused" freelancers earning 27% more on average than their "unfused" peers.

Superfused, for the purposes of this study, were defined as freelancers who self-identified as using combined skill sets, and who spent time on a range of diverse activities. So superfuse your skill set, so that when you're ready to leave, you can show your employer what you're capable of.

Give Notice

Treat this as the beginning of your freelance career, because in essence, that's what it is. So plan every move carefully—from timing your departure to how to tell your boss why you're leaving. Following are some concrete tips on how to make your announcement professional without burning any bridges.

- *Give ample notice:* It's advisable to give more than the standard two weeks' notice because the reason for your leaving is more unconventional than simply taking another position. A month's notice is more appropriate in this situation. This shows your boss that you've given thought to the situation in which you're leaving them and are giving ample time for them to find someone to replace you.
- *Give specific thanks:* Thank your boss for her investment in you as an employee. When possible, think of a specific instance or two when she was personally involved in helping you grow as a person or employee. Let her know how much you've valued her hand in guiding your career to this point, and that it's given you the foundation to have the courage to step out on your own. Please, make this genuine. People can sense when you're being disingenuous, so if you can't think of one good thing that your boss has done for you, it's best to give a more general thanks: "I've learned so much working here, lessons that I know will help in ways I probably can't even imagine right now as I step out on my own." And leave it at that.
- *Tie up loose ends:* Do everything in your power to make the transition as smooth as possible from you to the person taking your position. Offer to train, assist, or stay late to finish a project when necessary. This shows your boss that you're the ultimate professional and are putting the needs of the firm—your current employer—front and center.
- *Take your boss to lunch:* Keeping in mind that you hope to get business from your current company, ask your boss to lunch to make your announcement. Treat it as a business meeting. Tell her that you'd like to speak with her about a private matter, and that you'd like to do it away from the office if possible. This

isn't necessary, of course, but it's a classy move. It gives you a chance to explain in detail why you're making this career move, to invite your boss to ask detailed questions about your decision, and to let her know in a non-pushy manner that you'd be happy to have the company as a client.

Tailored Offer

Ask your boss for her business—in the form of a tailored offer just for her. It can be as brief or detailed as you like. When deciding on how detailed to make it, take into account what you know about your boss and your firm: how she likes to be approached, what's most important to her, what you know the firm needs, what its goals are, and so forth.

At a minimum, give your boss a highlight of your proposed offer—again, one that is tailored specifically to the firm. Let her know she can try you out on a trial basis if she wants, just to see how things go.

This lets her know you've given serious thoughts to her needs, how you can help her achieve her goals, and that you're a true professional because you planned it all out so well.

What to Do after You Leave

Whether or not you've gotten a firm offer of work from your previous employer, there are two things you should do after you leave to "massage" this lead on an on-going basis.

Send Thank-You Notes

Yeah, you know, the old-fashioned kind that you buy from the stationery store and have to pull out an actual pen to write on. Hardly any one does this anymore—and for that reason alone, it'll make you stand out. And it's another classy move you add to the way you'll be remembered. When in doubt, select high-quality, classy stationery.

Send them to your boss and those you worked with personally, thanking them for all their advice, help, insights, friendship, and well wishes. Keep your notes simple, thoughtful (and funny if that's part of who you are—you can never go wrong with funny), and to the point.

Stay in Touch

This can be done via social media like LinkedIn, or via e-mail. For example, if you notice a coworker posted on LinkedIn that they got a promotion, chime in and congratulate. If you notice that the merger your ex-boss worked on for six months finally went through, reference the article and send it along with a congratulatory note. Or if you know that your ex-firm has had a hard time filling a key position and someone you met might fit the bill, pass it along to key department heads. The point is to be helpful, while staying top of mind.

3. Use Cheap Gig Sites

Nothing gets a debate raging among freelancers more than when you discuss rates, which often involve what some consider "cheap gig" sites, such as Fiverr.com, Upwork.com, and Guru.com. But these types of talent-sourcing sites play a huge part in the freelance economy, as the 2013 merger of freelance labor marketplaces oDesk and Elance (rebranded as Upwork) illustrate.

Stephane Kasriel, who was named the chief executive of Upwork in 2015, the world's largest freelance talent marketplace, believes that the company will hit $10 billion in annual revenue within six years. And her belief is not unfounded, as she explained: "The entire freelance market is moving online. . . . Within a few years we are going to go from having 50,000 freelancers on the online marketplace to 500,000 independent workers online."

With Upwork's ability for employers to hire freelancers on the go via a mobile app, or in minutes via their talent platform, it's easy to see why Kasriel's projections are attainable.

Five Reasons to Consider Freelance Talent Marketplaces

Major marketplaces such as Upwork, Fiverr, and Guru are the hunting grounds to which many independent professionals turn to get their freelance careers off the ground. While these types of sites are routinely slammed for things like being stocked with employers looking for cheap labor, they remain highly popular. Following are five reasons that shed some light on why these online job marketplaces remain go-to sites for freelance job seekers.

1. Overcome Fear

Remember the discussion in Chapter 1 about fear—fear of failure and fear of success? Fear is perhaps the leading reason many people abandon the idea of freelancing altogether. This is rooted in lack of confidence—in your skill, yourself, your abilities.

Getting jobs on "cheapie sites" can be a great way to get over your fears. For example, the whole premise behind Fiverr and other sites like it is that you can "Get stuff done for just $5!"

No one expects the moon and the stars for $5—well the vast majority don't anyway. But of course, you treat the job as you would one that was paying you whatever your market rate is, get some great feedback, and probably land a repeat customer.

This can boost your confidence immensely, which gives you the incentive you need to go after your next job and your next and the one after that. Before you know it, your fears have dissipated. Heck, you're nailing this freelance thing! It's fun! You can do it! You might not have even tried if you started out targeting clients who pay market rates because it might have been too intimidating.

See how these kinds of freelance marketplaces can work in your favor when it comes to helping you get over your fears?

2. Get Project Experience

If you've never freelanced before and don't have a portfolio of work, a freelance marketplace is a great way to get a few jobs under your belt and start building one. Over and beyond gaining actual project experience though, you'll learn so much more: what to expect as far as work flow is concerned, the differences in client work styles, what's normal as far as turnaround times, and what to expect in the way of interaction and feedback.

There are so many kinds of projects that there's no way to predict what will happen with 100 percent certainty. This is another fear you may have. How will I know what to do? When? Will I finish on time? What kinds of questions will the client ask? What if I don't know the answer? What if they want to expand the project? Should I charge more for that? . . . The list goes on and on and on.

The only way to get answers to your questions, the only way to get project experience is to, well, work on projects. Again, it can be a lot less intimidating when a client finds you in a freelance marketplace and offers you a job, instead of you pitching him for a market-rate job.

3. Clients Come to You

What an ego boost to have clients seeking you out instead of the other way around. Now, this doesn't mean you don't have to be pro-active in going after clients on these types of sites. You do!

However, after winning a few projects—or maybe just because of your unique skill set—you could have clients knocking at your virtual door instead of the other way around.

How's that for an ego boost!

4. Crystalize Policies

As stated previously, there are many different kinds of projects. Even experienced freelancers can struggle with setting up their policies and procedures and sticking with them. But with each project you learn how to:

- Set deadlines and turnaround times
- Have clients submit work

- Handle requests for changes
- Charge for add-ons
- Set billing and payment policies
- Hire and pay other freelancers

None of these will be set in stone when you first start out, except maybe your billing and payment policies and how to have clients submit work. That's because you probably won't know what works until you've gotten a few jobs under your belt. Even then, as you gain more experience and your freelance business grows, policies and procedures are likely to change.

5. One-Stop Shopping

There's an old expression that goes, "The only thing worse than having a job is looking for one." Freelance marketplaces can cut down on your prospecting because they're like an online Walmart when it comes to finding clients. You can find every kind of prospect you could possibly want there, from one-person start-ups to *Fortune* 500 companies and everything in between. They're in every niche—finance, legal, tech, medicine, you name it.

Instead of wondering where to look for clients, you can get right down to crafting your proposals and sending them out to prospects—and possibly landing jobs that much sooner.

FREELANCER TIP

When using these sites, be sure to make them work for you, instead of against your long-term career aspirations. Many who are frustrated with these sites often lament that it keeps them stuck in low-paying gigs. A lot of this goes back to lack of self-confidence and fear. Remember this and the steps discussed in Chapter 1 for overcoming it.

While many—mostly experienced—freelancers knock "cheapie sites" like the freelance marketplaces mentioned here (and many others), there is a place for them.

How to Leverage Freelance Marketplaces

Many have leveraged freelance marketplaces to create successful freelance businesses—and it's because they took advantage of the benefits these types of sites offer, instead of getting mired in the negativity associated with them.

Complete Your Profile

This is akin to a resume for a full-time job. Not only should your profile be letter perfect, it should clearly demonstrate who you are, what your specific skill set is, and how you can help the client (many freelancers forget this part).

Common Profile Mistakes

No photo: Even though it's the web, people still do business with people—with people they know, like, and trust (remember the discussion on networking through chambers of commerce?). Show prospects your face so they know who they're doing business with. The shot should be professional, cropped correctly, and in focus.

Oversharing: This is no time to overshare. Don't include personal information such as marital status, age, why you started freelancing, and so on.

Incomplete profiles: Some freelancers set up their accounts and put in the bare minimum. They intend to go back and fill it in completely, but never do. An incomplete profile says as much about you as a complete one—namely whether you care enough to sell yourself to potential employers.

When you sign up, be sure to make your profile as complete as possible, including verified credentials and tested skills.

Outdated profiles: Many freelancers who may do a great job of putting up a profile initially never go back to update it. You should constantly freshen your profile, adding new samples of your work, positive feedback obtained from recent clients, new skills you've learned, and any other relevant information.

Not only does this illustrate to potential clients what you can do, it shows them that you're still active. This is important because there are a lot of "dead" profiles on these sites.

FREELANCER TIP

Many people used to include a "Hobbies/Interest" section at the end of their resume. For some recruiters, this can be a starting point to gaining insight into the personality of a candidate. So if you have an interesting hobby (for instance, you have run ten marathons in ten countries), include it. You never know. Don't include hobbies that some may consider ethically questionable, such as big-game hunting.

Be Proactive

The more you bid, the better chance you have of landing a gig, so bid frequently. Many jobs are never awarded on these sites (according to some estimates, 40 percent or more). What this means is, a lot of your proposals will never result in a job, no matter how talented you are or well put together your proposal is.

Don't be discouraged. It's a numbers game. Keep this in mind when you decide on your bidding frequency. The more you bid, the more jobs you win, and the quicker your earnings will rise.

Customize Your Proposals

Make your proposals as targeted to the specific gig at hand as possible.

Toke Kruse, the self-described owner of several businesses and CEO of Billy's Billing, uses Elance to hire freelancers. He sums this point up this way:

> Before making a bid on a project, it can be very helpful to communicate with the prospective client, to clarify what he or she needs. . . .
>
> In sending such a communication, introduce yourself briefly, tell the client that you're interested in the project, and ask for information or clarifications you need in order to make a fair bid. A good client (one you're likely to be happy to work for) will appreciate your questions and the professionalism they indicate. Be sure to be very clear and concise.

Employers receive tons of responses when they post jobs. Many of them are from lazy freelancers who send the same correspondence to many prospects. If yours is specific and targeted to the job at hand, you have a much better chance of catching a prospect's eye.

FREELANCER TIP

Research what employers want. For example, Upwork's blog often features employers who give specifics about what makes them hire one freelancer as opposed to another. Many of these are concrete examples you can act on. Take these golden nuggets and turn them to your advantage.

Don't Give Up

As previously stated, freelance marketplaces are unpopular with a lot of freelancers and to be completely honest, the ratio of junk jobs to good can seem like 500 to 1. But by filtering out the junk and focusing on the good stuff, you can make the sites work for you. As a rule of thumb, give yourself three to four months of solid bidding before you decide to rule them out.

The previous tips give you a great head start on what to expect and how to increase your chance of landing gigs, especially the one about customizing your proposals.

How to Retain Existing Clients

According to the Pareto principle, 80 percent of your jobs will come from 20 percent of your clients. It's important to understand this wisdom because you can wind up in the trap that many freelancers fall into—chasing new clients instead of servicing existing ones.

Following are six of the easiest ways to get more work from existing clients.

1. Create an Auto Follow-Up System

This can be as simple as including a note with each completed project reminding clients of your availability. This is pretty passive, but better than nothing.

A more proactive approach would be to schedule a follow-up call or send out a follow-up e-mail a couple of days after you turn in a project to see if the client has any back-end questions or concerns. This makes it a warm touch, instead of a cold, badgering one, and it gives you the perfect opportunity to ask specifically about previous work:

"Hello, Joanne, just checking in to see if you had any questions about that last job."

[Listen to client remarks and respond appropriately.] Then end with . . .

"I remember you mentioned wanting to get started on the Temple project. I know you said you were busy, but I have some ideas for that and I can get started on it for you. If we get started within the next week, I can have it done for you before the holidays officially start."

See how smooth that is? You ask for the job by wrapping it in a benefit for the client, for instance, getting a job done so she can enjoy her holidays stress-free.

By making it your "company policy" to follow up with a phone call or e-mail forty-eight hours after a project is finished, you give yourself a reason to "touch" the client again while your memory is still warm with them.

2. Simple Reminders

If it's been a while since you've worked with a client, get in touch and remind him that you're still around. This can be done by phone, e-mail, newsletter, or social media. Just a quick shout-out can do wonders.

"Hey, Joe, it's Sally here from Lightning Fast Accounting. I hope all has been going well. I know it's been awhile since we've been in touch, but it's almost time for quarterly P&Ls to be generated. There've been a couple of sticky IRS changes that have come down the pike that are a thorn in the side to small business like yours, and I was just wondering if you're up to speed. I'm around if you have any questions, so let me know if you need me to generate your quarterly P&Ls, okay?"

"New IRS changes? I didn't know that? Maybe I should give her a call," Joe thinks.

As an aside, this is where really knowing your client base comes in handy. You know their pain points—what they're likely to most need help with. Zeroing in on these can increase your chance of getting more work from existing clients.

3. Ask for Referrals

Ask for the referral. It's the simplest thing to do, and if a client is happy with your work, the vast majority will be happy to refer you. But they won't if you don't ask, and it's not because they don't want to, it's because they're busy handling their own workload. It just may not occur to them to refer you—that is, unless and until you ask.

A quick, "Hey, Mary, do you know of anyone else who could use my services? I'd really appreciate it if you would give me their contact info, or pass mine along to them."

Make it a habit to do this with every one of your clients. Again, systemize the process to make it an ingrained habit. How? One way is to include a feedback form with each project turned in. One of the things you could put on it is, "If you know of anyone who can use our services, please forward their contact info."

Asking for referrals can seem a bit pushy to some freelancers, but think of it this way: Your existing clients already know, like, and trust you and your work. So you have to be doing a lot right.

Hold on to that . . . and forge ahead.

4. Bundle Services

Many times, clients will hire you to do a project and be blissfully unaware of the complete range of services you provide—even when they're right there on your website. It's your job to make them aware of all that you have to offer. One way to do this is to bundle services.

For example, if you're a wedding photographer, you could offer an "engagement package of photos" for the upcoming bride and groom. What's this? Many engaged couples want to document some special moments leading up to their wedding. You could offer to photograph them in their home, or on a romantic date in the park, or walking through the snow hand in hand—precious moments when it's just the two of them that they can reflect on before they get married.

How many engaged couples do you think would know about this service unless you told them? By bundling it with your wedding photography services, you introduce them to it, and they'll likely tell their friends, who'll tell their friends—and the snowball of referrals start rolling in.

Even if only 5, 10, or 15 percent of your customers take advantage of a bundled service offering, it can mean a big difference to your bottom line at the end of the year (depending on your pricing).

5. Expand Service Offerings

Have your clients been asking for services that you don't offer? Or, do you notice that others in your niche offer a service that you don't offer? Then maybe it's time to offer it. The goal is the same as with the bundled service offering—to increase the value of each order.

6. Teach to Earn

What does this mean? Educating your clients by showcasing your knowledge. In this digital age, old marketing techniques don't work. The buying public—B2B and B2C consumers are overwhelmed with information. Most have already done their due diligence in some form or another. Buyers don't want or need to be sold to. What they want is to be educated. This is why educational marketing is the name of the game these days. Some effective ways to do this are:

- *Blogging*: Posting timely, relevant content that solves problems for your targeted niche.
- *Newsletter marketing*: Sending out actionable tips; links to your informative blog posts; keeping prospects abreast of relevant industry news and happenings.
- *Case studies*: Showing how your product/service solved a client's problem.
- *Seminars*: You can hold monthly, quarterly, semiannual, or annual seminars that speak to the pain points of your particular niche. A good way to make a maximum impact with seminars is to thoroughly research what it is prospects in your

niche are worried or concerned about. Send out questionnaires asking them what issues they'd like to be covered. Then build a seminar around that.

Not only does this give you a legitimate reason to reach out to many prospects at once, it sets you up as an industry leader, helps you identify new trends, and cultivates opportunities for new work.

An educated prospect is an informed prospect, and an informed prospect is much more likely to buy. If you do these six things, you'll cut down the sales cycle into a much shorter timeframe, and increase profits at the same time.

Chapter 8

Structuring Your Workday

If you're just starting out your freelance business, expect to spend 75 to 80 percent of your time marketing, because if you're not marketing, you're not bringing in business. And if you don't have clients, nothing else you do will matter.

Allocating Time

Following is a formula you can use as a brand-new freelancer to effectively allocate your time from nine to five.

Direct Marketing: 9 A.M. to 1 P.M.

Direct marketing is any kind of marketing you do to reach out and touch a customer. It can be e-mailing, cold-calling, attending a networking event, and so on.

Break: 1 P.M. to 1:30 P.M.

You're excited. You have so much to do. You feel overwhelmed. It can be tempting to work nonstop. Don't do it. Many freelancers never build a break into their workday. But you need to eat, rest your eyes, stretch, and so on. From the beginning get in the habit of doing this, even if it's for only half an hour a day. You deserve it and your body needs it.

Indirect Marketing: 1:30 P.M. to 4 P.M.

This is marketing that may not garner an immediate sale but is part of your overall marketing strategy. For example, you might create an industry report to put on your website as a free download in order to encourage subscribers to sign up for your newsletter. You might write blog posts and schedule them to go out next week.

Getting Up to Speed: 4 P.M. to 5 P.M.

There is always something to learn when you go out on your own: how to update a blog in WordPress, what makes an effective Facebook ad, how to create eBook covers, what the latest industry report revealed and how it affects your service offerings, what search engine optimization (SEO) means, and so on. It's important to schedule time in your workday to improve and add to your freelancing skills.

This schedule will change, of course, as you bring clients on and you have to work on projects, but this is a basic timetable you can use starting on Day 1 to guide you in allocating your time effectively.

Twenty-Four Hours Is Enough

Ever heard of Parkinson's law? It states, "Work expands to fill the time available for its completion."

The "law" was satirically proposed in 1955 by British political analyst and historian Cyril Northcote Parkinson, who was criticizing the British Admiralty. The Admiralty was growing while the number of sailors and ships under its care was decreasing. Parkinson's law explained why: the bureaucracy found work for its civil servants to do, even if that work wasn't really necessary. Since then the law has been applied by the business world as a keen insight into the functioning of large, often bloated, organizations.

The law makes clear that it's not that you're lacking in time—we all get the same twenty-four hours in a day—but you need to be more judicious in how you use your time.

Twenty-four hours . . . it's enough.

How to Set Up Your Office

As you head to the couch to catch the evening news with your favorite snack, you stifle the urge to do a little jig because today was your last day at the office, and the need for those two-inch, wedge-heeled pumps that were your wardrobe staple no longer exists.

You peer at your bunny slippers as you prop your feet on the coffee table and wiggle your toes in them. The bunny's head bobs back and forth and you let out a laugh—a ridiculous, I'm-glad-I'm-here-by-myself laugh, because you're so happy. You are now officially a lone wolf—a freelance business owner. And your office is right down the hall.

Or in that corner in the living room.

Or that space under the staircase where the desk is.

Or in that nook in the dining room.

Until now, you've been working all over the house, but now that you're an official business, you need a more permanent space.

You look at your bunny feet and ask the fluffy creature, as if you expect a real answer, "Jeez, where will my official office be? And how the heck should I set it up so I can get work done every day?"

Bunny doesn't have the answer, so here is some practical advice.

Natural Light

If possible, locate your primary work area near a source of natural light. It's vital for productivity and health. How vital? Consider the following from a study on light in the workplace reported on in the *Journal of Clinical Sleep Medicine.*

Light is the most important synchronizing agent for the brain and body [and] proper synchronization of your internal biological rhythms with the earth's daily rotation has been shown to be essential for health. Office workers with more light exposure at the office had longer sleep duration, better sleep quality, more physical activity and better quality of life compared to office workers with less light exposure in the workplace.

The study also found that daylight from side windows almost vanishes if a workstation is located twenty to twenty-five feet from windows, so make sure your desk is located within this distance to maximize light exposure.

Noise

You want your workspace to be located in a space as quiet as possible. While you may like working with music or don't mind other types of noises, what happens when you have to take a business call or are trying to communicate over Skype?

Set up your home office in a spot where noise will not be a distraction, not only for you, but for the people with whom you may be interacting on the phone or on your computer.

Comfort

You will spend a great amount of time in your home office, so you want it to be as comfortable as possible. Invest in a good, ergonomically comfortable chair to prevent back strain; an ergonomic keyboard to minimize wrist and muscle strain, and related problems; a computer monitor that reduces eye strain; and an ergonomic foot rest to ease leg and lower-back issues, and help with circulation.

Privacy

Where possible, set up your office in a space that's private so that if you need to close a door to get some work done, you won't have others traipsing through your space. If you have a dedicated space such as a spare bedroom, you'll be able to close up at the end of the workday without having to pack up.

Storage

Even if you operate a virtual, paperless business, there will always be some peripherals that you need: extra computer battery, headphones, pens, pencils, and other office supplies. So storage, even if it's just a drawer, is important.

> **FREELANCER TIP**
>
> You don't have to buy new. Check used office supply stores and thrift outlets to save. As well, look at online sites such as Craigslist for inexpensive office furnishings.

Flat Space

This one area many freelancers don't think about. You need flat space, even if it's only to fit the book that always seems to be on your desk, your coffee cup and lunch tray, your eyeglass case, or for that time once a month when you print out and go over your financial statements.

You may not need a lot, but you do need it, so when you're setting up your office, make sure you have some dedicated flat space.

Climate

Before you decide to set up in that corner in the basement or by that storm window in the attic, make sure that it's comfortable year round. Is it insulated? You don't want to be able to see your breath in the winter and sweat bullets in the summer because the space is not properly outfitted for proper temperature control year round.

Zen

If you need purple furry balls hanging from the ceiling to feel creative, then hang some purple furry balls from the ceiling. If bright orange pillows make you happy, then by all means buy bright orange pillows.

The point is to make your office comfortable for *you*. You're going to be spending a lot of time there. It should be a place where you feel happy and at peace.

Organization

No matter where your home office is located—a corner in your living room, or in a spare, separate bedroom—the key to staying productive in it is to stay organized.

It's easy for messiness and chaos to creep in, especially when you get busy, and especially if you're lucky enough to have set up in a separate room that you can just close the door to. But don't. When designing your space, create an organizational system that keeps everything in its place so you can easily locate it.

> **FREELANCER TIP**
>
> When you're in business, time is money and wasting forty-five minutes to an hour or more each day looking for things can add up to a chunk of money you're not making. For example, let's say you bill an average of $50 an hour. If you waste an hour a day because you're unorganized, that's costing you almost $1,100 per month, which translates into almost $13,000 per year.
>
> Would you get organized if someone agreed to pay you $13,000? This is how important organization is to the success of your freelance business. So get—and stay—organized.

How to Use Time-Blocking to Earn More

Time-blocking is just another way to get organized. To get things done, you can use a process that we'll call ICE—identify, categorize, execute.

Identify

Ascertain what's most important to get done. This should be aligned with your financial goals, which will be driven by your marketing strategy, so most likely—especially in the beginning of your business—this will be some kind of direct or indirect marketing activity.

Categorize

After you've identified what you want to accomplish, it's time to split your tasks into categories. This will help you get them done more efficiently. For example, remember how we time-blocked our nine-to-five day into direct marketing activities, indirect marketing activities, and getting up to speed. Grouping like activities keeps you from feeling scattered. It keeps you . . . guess what? Organized!

Execute

Once you've catalogued your activities into like groups, then all you have to do is execute. Be sure to use productivity tools such as Hootsuite, Google Calendar, and Toggl to help you stay on track.

You'll find that no time-blocked day will ever flow exactly as you have it outlined. But that doesn't mean resorting to flying by the seat of your pants. That's a surefire way to start wasting hours—and costing you money.

FREELANCER TIP

An article at Inc.com, "Richard Branson Is Right: Time Is the New Money," states: "Give people control over their time, and they will build a great company, not *for* you, but *with* you. In the Participation Age, time is the new money." This is, indeed, the participation age, and as a freelancer, time is your currency—the currency you use to build a company, not for someone else, but for yourself.

You should be able to look at every hour of your day and know what you need to be working on. This is why time-blocking is so effective. It keeps you from wasting two hours on Facebook, half an hour talking to your girlfriend who called in the middle of the day, and another hour slogging through e-mail.

Four Ways to Avoid Distractions

Distractions are one of the hardest things to avoid as a freelancer, especially if you've never freelanced before and are used to the structure of a nine-to-five job.

It can take many freelancers years to bring some structure to their business. Some never do. They give up on their dream of freelancing, thinking that they just didn't have what it takes to make it. But sometimes, it really is as simple as avoiding distractions so you can maximize each hour of your day.

Following are four things you should get in the habit of doing from day one. They will keep distractions to a minimum, and you'd be amazed at how much you will accomplish in a short period.

Time-Block Your Days

As discussed previously, organization is essential to maximum efficiency. Employing a method such as time-blocking will not only keep you on track during the day, it will also help keep you focused. It is easy to become distracted if you don't have a set schedule to your day, so remember: ICE—identify, categorize, execute.

Set Defined Work Hours

There's nothing "free" about freelancing—you have to put in the work to live the dream. Setting defined work hours—just as you would when you had a nine-to-five job, will greatly increase your productivity.

"It takes the fun out of freelancing!"

"I don't want to!"

"I'll make up the time."

"That's not really freelancing."

Some or all of these may be your reaction to having a defined work schedule as a freelancer, but if you don't set distinct work hours, following is what's likely to happen. You'll:

1. Wind up not putting in the hours necessary to build a successful freelance business
2. Become discouraged because jobs aren't coming in
3. Find that you're less structured in other areas of your business as well

Just because you set regular work hours does not mean they have to be nine to five. If you're not a morning person, you can set your hours to be 11 A.M. to 7 P.M., or noon to 10 P.M.

Conversely, if you're a night owl and/or have kids, work from 9 P.M. to 5 A.M., or midnight to 6 A.M.; then stop, get the kids dressed and off to school, and put in three more hours from 9 A.M. to noon.

This is where the freedom—and beauty—of freelancing is realized. You can build your work around your life, instead of the other way around.

Stay Off Facebook and Twitter

With Facebook blooping, and Twitter pinging, and e-mail zinging, it can be hard to focus if you work with the Internet on. There are too many distractions. It's one of the leading causes of lost productivity in the American workforce.

With no worries of a boss cruising by your desk who might see your open Facebook, Amazon, and Instagram pages, it's even more tempting to goof off. You're free—free to surf until your heart is content . . . or until your bank account drops to zero.

Log off. Log off. Log off. For your sanity, and your pocketbook.

Work in Bursts

Even when you time-block, it can be tough to stay focused. One thing that can help is to work in defined bursts, for example, focus on one task for fifteen minutes, take a five-minute break (your eyes need a break anyway), then do another fifteen minutes.

Block out all distractions and focus on nothing but that specific task at hand. It hyperfocuses you. You'd be amazed at what you can accomplish by working in this manner.

How to Handle Dry Spells

You've been rocking and rolling. Projects have been rolling in at a steady pace, and a couple of times you've even outsourced jobs to other freelancers because you've been so busy and are thinking about scaling up your business.

Then, a week goes by. Nothing new.

Another few days fly by. "Hmm, what's going on?" you think.

Then eight more days go by—you know exactly how many days it's been because you've been looking at your empty calendar. There've been no projects, no proposals to put together—not even a nibble. Nothing.

Does e-mail still work?

Did you forget to pay your cell phone bill?

Have your social media accounts been hacked?

You quickly Google your name/company name. Did somebody say something bad on the web about you?

What's going on? Where have all the jobs gone? You're almost in full-blown panic mode.

Hold on. Slow your roll. You've hit your first dry spell. Welcome to one of the most common phases of freelancing. It's completely normal. It happens to every freelancer at some point, and you will get through it.

Following are six things you can do to not only weather dry spells but use them to your advantage. As you will see, they can be a blessing in disguise, especially if you learn how to recognize them and use the time to refresh, reboot, and move forward with even more determination.

Don't Panic

If you're new to freelancing, a dry spell can totally freak you out because the bills still have to be paid. It's hard to make rational decisions in panic mode. Calm down and recognize this for what it is—a dry spell. Nothing more, nothing less.

Others have weathered it, and you will too. Don't start second-guessing yourself and wondering if you made the right career choice. You did the upfront work, remember—business plan, marketing plan, strategizing, padding your bank account with savings.

So relax, relate, and release. You've got this!

Don't Stop Marketing

One of the first things many freelancers do is look for ways to cut expenses when things dry up. This is not a time to do this. If you've run your numbers and have budgeted to spend a certain amount per month on marketing, then continue to do so. Think about it this way: How is slowing down or stopping your marketing going to bring in gigs?

Again, it's just a dry spell. If you disappear from your target market's radar just because they're not responding right now, you won't be visible when they do need what you offer again. So stick to your marketing schedule.

Double Down on Marketing

Keep doing any paid marketing that's working and that you've budgeted for, and double down on free and low-cost methods.

For example, if your normal routine is to make five cold calls per day, make ten. If you normally mail out 200 postcards per month and can find a deal, mail out 400. If you normally only attend the afternoon chamber of commerce meeting, go to the morning one as well.

The key is to increase your visibility, not sit back in a corner and doubt yourself. That sort of thing can lead to all kinds of negative outcomes: depression, lack of confidence, and decreased motivation, to name a few.

So keep busy putting yourself out there. Something will shake loose sooner or later—guaranteed.

Evaluate Your Business

If things suddenly dry up and you've been pounding the pavement but nothing materializes in a month or two, it's time to look at your business model. Following are five areas to assess.

1. Pricing: Is it in line with what others are offering? Is it too high? Too low? Being the cheapest is not always the best thing. It could be costing you business because potential clients don't believe you can deliver the value a higher-priced competitor ostensibly offers.
2. Delivery: Are you taking too long?
3. Services: Are your customers looking for more of a one-stop shop, yet you only offer limited services?
4. Competition: Did some new innovation come down the pike that you don't know about or aren't up on? What are your competitors doing that you're not?
5. Quality: Is the quality that clients want, need, and expect there? Be honest with yourself here.

Go through your business with a fine-toothed comb and make adjustments where necessary.

Learn a New Skill

If you're satisfied that all is well with your business, take this downtime to learn a new skill that you can add to your service list or that will help you handle backend office functions more efficiently. It's something you've been wanting to do anyway, right? Now that you have some free hours in the day, it's a great way to invest that time in your business for long-term payoff.

Take a Vacation

Again, if you're satisfied that it's just a dry spell and all your systems are still in place, then take the time to rest. You got your freelance business off the ground. You've had clients, so you know there's a need for what you offer. Things will turn around. So take some time to kick back, relax, and rejuvenate your brain, so that when those calls do start coming in, you're refreshed and ready to get back on the rollercoaster ride that is freelancing.

Chapter 9

Working with Clients

Great clients are worth their weight in gold. You live for them, treasure them, and wish that a whole planet could be populated with them. But you must learn how to screen out the bad aliens to get to the cream-of-the-croppers who make you drool as a freelancer.

How to Vet/Screen Clients

Following are some measures you can take to vet potential clients.

Determine If They Are Your Ideal Client

When a prospect contacts you, not only is she assessing you for the job, you're assessing her as well. Most freelancers are so happy to have a prospect on the hook that they forget this. It's normal, but you have to learn to put that initial excitement in check.

Now it's time to put all that research and time and thought that went into your business plan to work. Remember when we discussed ideal clients versus peripheral ones? One of the first questions you should be asking is, "Does this prospect fit my ideal client mold?"

All your products and services are built around servicing a certain type of client, catering to her needs, solving a defined set of problems.

If a prospect falls outside of these parameters, it can be a nightmare for you because the systems, process, and services you offer aren't set up to provide what they need.

This means it can take you longer to complete a project, lowering your overall profit because it's not something you designed your business to provide. Then there's the stress and uncertainty that goes along with the fear that maybe you're not giving the client what she wants.

This is why you need to start with this question. If a client is not a fit for you, pass. In fact, you might want to set up a referral system with other freelancers just for situations like this. While you may be focused on the dollars walking out the door, think of all the ones you could be blocking by all that could go wrong when you work with a client who is not part of your defined target market.

"But what if I can do the job? Sure, it's not my ideal client, but I can do that job with my eyes closed. I know I could."

If you know that you can provide the value that a client is looking for—even though the client may fall outside the scope of your ideal prospect, then by all means, go for it.

While you should always strive to work with your ideal client, you have to be realistic too. Your ideal clients are your foundation; they're the ones who are going to propel your business to the next level. But you need to keep the lights on and food in your belly—and clients who come along who don't fit your ideal profile but are willing to fork over your fee are good too.

Create a Client Questionnaire

A client questionnaire is a great way to achieve this goal. Keep it handy so that when a prospect contacts you, you can have all the qualifying questions you want to ask right in front of you. Some questions you might want to ask are:

- What type of business is your company?
- What is your goal for/with this project?

- Who's the end-customer for this product/service?
- What timeframe are you looking at?
- How do you like to be contacted?
- How often do you like to be updated?
- Who will be the primary contact?
- Have you ever worked with a freelancer before?
- Do you have existing materials you can pass along to me to help with the project?
- What's the budget?
- How do you pay and what are your payment terms?

Once the prospect gives you a company name, you can Google other important details such as how big/small his company is, how long he's been in business, who his competitors are, and so forth. The information you want to get from your questionnaire is stuff you can't find online. It will give you more insight into what he expects from you if you decide to work together.

When you question a prospect, it shouldn't be done in a rapid-fire, "I'm interviewing you" style. Stay conversational and phrase questions in a way that puts the prospect at ease. Make it clear that you're trying to understand what *they* want so you can deliver. This is what your questionnaire is designed to accomplish.

Online Screening

A client contacts you out of the blue. She needs her website completely overhauled. She needs it within five days, and the job pays $5,000. Can you get started right away?

Sure. Fast work is your specialty. It's a pretty simple site, and you can get the job done in three days you tell her. All you need is a 50 percent deposit, and the remaining 50 percent upon completion to release the site to them.

Silence. You never hear from her again.

When an unknown prospect contacts you out of the blue, usually with some type of large order, and she or he is unwilling to pay a deposit, it's a red flag. This is why it's important to do some online research. You'd be amazed at what you can find out just by Googling a prospect's e-mail address (an often overlooked, simple research method). Sometimes you'll find pages of info about how they've scammed other freelancers.

Other methods of online screening include checking social media profiles, online industry forums, the Better Business Bureau, freelancer warning and scam sites, and Dun & Bradstreet (D&B), a commercial data company that provides information on a business's credit history, among a host of other info.

If you can't find anything about the prospect online, don't proceed, or at least proceed with extreme caution. It's practically impossible to be a legitimate business these days without some kind of web footprint.

Trust Your Gut

Sometimes your gut screams loud and clear for you not to take on a job, even when it seems that the prospect may be an ideal fit.

Bad clients tend to niggle from the start. You may not know why, but if you ever work with one and have your gut proven right, when you look back, you'll almost always be able to say, "Something told me from the very beginning not to take on this project."

Your gut is one of the most valuable screening tools you have as a freelancer. Listen to it.

"Saying no to others means you are saying yes to yourself, which is ultimately of even greater benefit to the ones you were saying no to."
—ED AND DEB SHAPIRO, PERSONAL DEVELOPMENT AND
MEDITATION TEACHERS AND COAUTHORS

When to Say "No"

No is one of the most powerful things you can say as a freelancer because it's grounded in a belief that there's enough work to go around and all you have to do is put your systems and processes in place and go out and get it. With this mindset at the forefront, following are some times when it's best to say no to a potential client.

If They're Disrespectful

Some clients act as if they're doing you a favor by giving you work. They speak to you and interact with you as if you're little better than a low-wage employee. There is no amount of money in the world worth dealing with this type of client. Saying no is a no-brainer.

If They Can't Afford You

If you come from a traditional job, you may come to freelancing with an employee mentality. It's a mindset of "Please choose me. I can do the job. I know I can."

One of the ways you may entice them to choose you is by competing on rate, being too willing to negotiate even when the market research you conducted shows that you're already competitively priced.

There are some clients who cannot afford you. This is fine. Have a bottom line that you are not willing to go below. If you don't, it can eat away at your self-worth. It can make you angry while you're completing the project. It can pave the way for doubting your worth. Rate, unlike what many believe, is not the most important factor prospects consider in the purchasing process. So when you think about violating your rate rule, consider the following. A study by ISPO News, "90 Percent of All Purchasing Decisions Are Made Subconsciously," found:

> 90 percent of all purchasing decisions are not made consciously, experts claim. Or put it this way: brands and products that evoke our emotions, like Apple, Coca-Cola or Nivea, always win. . . . "A major part of our brain is busy with automatic processes, not conscious thinking. A lot of emotions and less cognitive activities happen," says behavioral economist George Loewenstein. . . . Thus,

our subconscious explains our consumer behavior better than our conscious.

As this research underscores, competing on rate is not as effective as you may think. In fact, it's a slippery slope that will lead to doing a lot of damage to your confidence as a freelancer.

The sooner you understand and accept that not everyone can afford you, the easier it'll be to say no.

If You Can't Do the Job

If the job is beyond your skill set, then of course, the ethical thing to do is to say no.

If the Client Doesn't Know What He Wants

If a client can't clearly communicate to you what he wants—even if you give him some defined guidelines to help clarify—then say no to the project. If you don't, you run the risk of never making him happy and possibly ruining your reputation, not to mention tearing your hair out. This kind of client can be difficult to work with because it is hard to please a customer when he doesn't know what he wants. Every time you think you've nailed the project, he comes up with a little change or a tweak.

Just say no. Save yourself the headache.

If You Just Don't Want To

If there's a type of project that you just don't enjoy working on—even if it is within your skill set—say no. You'll be doing the client a disservice by taking it on, not to mention what it will do to your spirit. Or, as discussed in the previous section on vetting clients, if your gut tells you it isn't the job for you, say no.

If You're Too Busy

If you can't meet a client's deadline, then say no. One of the things that can easily ruin your reputation is not meeting deadlines. Many times, the deadline is the exact reason clients outsource a project. They may not have the in-house resources to cover it, so they'll look for an outside source—like you—to deliver . . . on time and within budget.

If you can negotiate a favorable deadline—great. But if there's any doubt that you'll be able to make it, say no because it may cost the client a lot of money on the back end when you don't deliver.

Keep the Door Open for Future Business

One of the best ways to say no to a prospect, yet still keep the door open for possible future work, is to explain and counter.

For example, if you're too busy to meet a client's deadline right now, you might say something like: "I'm working on [current project] right now and there's no way I could do your project justice until this job is done. However, if you can be a bit more flexible with the deadline, I can get started on Thursday of next week."

Explaining and countering lets the client know that you are eager to work with her, and that you'll give her project the same amount of time and dedication as the work you're currently doing—if she can just work with you.

Even if she's not able to agree to your terms, she'll know why you turned her down.

Also, go the extra mile and follow up when you are free. This demonstrates follow-through and professionalism. Even if the last project has been outsourced to another freelancer, she may have something else you can get started on.

Freelancing and Contracts

If you ever watch the popular television show *Judge Judy*, you've probably seen the judge hold up a piece of paper—a contract, a lease, a handwritten IOU, etc.—and say to a plaintiff or defendant: "I work within the confines of this piece of paper. This is your contract. If it's not in here, it doesn't exist."

While many freelancers work without contracts for years, it's not advisable. A contract is more than just a legal document; it gets you and your client on the same page about what's expected, when, and how.

You're not just a freelancer. You need to scrap that mentality before it takes hold. You're a business, and you need to formalize that relationship with each client you bring on. A contract does this. It sends a message loud and clear that you have your freelance house in order, that you're a professional. You expect to be treated as such, and only the best can be expected by and from you.

Preparing Your Freelance Contract

As mentioned previously, a contract can be as simple as a hand-written IOU. It doesn't have to be long or complicated at all. In fact, the shorter the better.

What any contract you prepare needs to be is precise, spelling out what's expected from both parties and what will happen if the terms are breached.

There are many online templates you can use. If you go this route, select one that is specific to your industry. You can always customize a boilerplate contract you find online, adding any stipulations and special circumstances as they relate to your business, product, or service.

While you don't have to pay an attorney to draft a contract, you should have one look it over to make sure that you haven't overlooked any unforeseen circumstances that could come back to haunt you later.

As mentioned in Chapter 4, sites such as LegalZoom.com, LawHelp.org, Nolo.com, and ProBono.net are also good sources to consult to find affordable legal help.

Some specifics you definitely want to cover in your contract are: deadlines, payment terms, and cancellation terms.

No-cost templates for various types of freelance contracts can be found on sites such as www.Upwork.com, www.Docracy.com, and www.TidyForms.com.

How to Set, Meet, and Beat Deadlines

One of the most important aspects of working with clients is hitting your deadlines. A big part of your reputation as a freelancer stands or falls on your ability to do this. In this section, we'll look at some tips and tricks for delivering on time.

You thought you had it all planned out, giving yourself plenty of time to complete the project. But here it is, twenty-four hours before the deadline, and you're stressed to the max wondering how in the heck you're ever going to deliver on time. If you pull an all-nighter, you have a shot, but you never want to be in this position again.

If you've been freelancing for a while, you probably recognize this scenario. If you're new and never want to experience it, following are four things you can do to always meet and beat deadlines.

Estimate Correctly from the Beginning

This can be hard to do when you're first starting out, but you should have some idea of how long a project is going to take. This is one of the things to determine during your market analysis, especially when you look at your competitors. Draw on this knowledge now.

Unless a client specifically states that it's a rush job, usually he'll agree with the timeframe you give him, especially if it's within industry accepted standards. If it's longer, you may need to justify why (e.g., we'll have to do a deeper analysis because there's not a lot of current research available).

Following are some factors to consider before agreeing to a firm deadline:

- *Type of project:* Based on your discussions with the client, is it relatively easy, or more complex?
- *Your experience:* Have you done this type of work before?
- *How you work:* At what pace do you normally work? Are you a fast typer, researcher, reader, interviewer? Are you organized? Are you able to stay hyperfocused for a defined period? Do you tire easily?
- *How busy you are:* How many projects do you have on tap right now? Is this a busy or slow time for you? How much time will you be able to devote to this project daily? Is it enough to meet the proposed deadline? If you even have an inkling that you might be pushing it if you agree to a certain deadline, ask for more time because Murphy's Law will almost certainly pay a visit. Just when you need everything to fall into place perfectly—and you see no reason why it shouldn't—something will go wrong. You can almost always count on it. So when in doubt it's always best to ask for extra time. After all, it never hurts to deliver early. In fact, it makes you look quite amazing!
- *Your ability to hire help:* If you're in a pinch, do you have a backup roster of available freelancers you can call on for help?

Build in Extra Time

Even if you know without a doubt that you can deliver a project within three days, tell the client you need four or five. Always, always, always get in the habit of building in extra time because of ol' man Murphy, as mentioned previously.

Also, extra time gives you peace of mind. If something does happen and you need an extra day or two, it's already built into the timeline.

Don't Procrastinate

Procrastination can literally make or break your freelance career. It's a habit you cannot afford.

One of the biggest reasons for procrastination is subconsciously, or consciously, not knowing how or where to start—even when you have a defined process in place. Many times, however, the creative process doesn't start . . . until you start. Even if what you're producing when you start is crap, maybe crap is what you need to wade through to get to the hidden gem you see in your mind's eye that is the final result.

So when you have a project on tap, sit down and get started. You will be amazed at how powerful this simple action is.

FREELANCER TIP

Some projects take unforeseen turns where the initial deadline becomes impossible to meet. For example, if a client changes the parameters of a project midstream, this may throw off your schedule. When this happens, assess whether you need to renegotiate the deadline because the terms you initially agreed to no longer apply.

Communicate with the Client

As soon as you realize you may be in danger of missing a deadline, it's imperative that you let your client know right away. Explain as succinctly as possible why the deadline is in jeopardy.

If it's because of something you did, be prepared to lose the job, the client, and get some negative blowback. Don't obsess over it, however. Look at it as a valuable lesson. While your goal should always be to never miss a deadline, you can recover from it if you do—if you learn from it by putting systems in place so that it's a rare, almost nonexistent occurrence.

Every project you complete gives you more insight into how to efficiently run your business. And if you make use of productivity tools such as the ones mentioned in Chapter 8, you can seamlessly track hours, see your project at a glance, keep your days organized, and archive everything related to it, so you finish on time and within budget.

They say that 90 percent of success in life is showing up. If that's true, the other 10 percent just may be showing up on time.

Getting Paid

There are two types of clients: those who intend to pay and those who don't. Thankfully, the vast majority of your clients will fall in the first group. After all, their reputation is on the line too, so they're not about to stiff you. Here are some tips on how to ensure that you get paid for every job you do.

Have Defined Payment Guidelines in Writing

Decide what payment options you accept and when you're to be paid. Let the client know this upfront. It should be part of your client contract, signed off on by both of you. This way, there are no surprises.

Get a Portion Upfront

Always get a portion of your payment upfront. Some industries have set policies about this. For example, a freelance writer may require 50 percent upfront, while a web designer may bill in thirds: a third upfront, a third once a preliminary design is done, and the final third once the project is completed.

An upfront payment lets you know that the prospect is serious, and it also establishes a line of trust between you. It also means you won't be on the hook for the whole price of the project if the client bails. It is particularly important to establish this practice with new clients. If they balk, you walk.

Perform Client Due Diligence

Vetting potential clients goes a long way in lessening the chance that you'll be stiffed on a project. It's one of the main reasons to vet, which is discussed in detail previously in this chapter.

Bill on a Set Schedule

Many times freelancers aren't paid because they're unorganized with their recordkeeping, which means they don't bill in a timely manner. Your client can be the sweetest, most wonderful client in the world, but if you don't send her a bill, you're highly unlikely to get a check in the mail or a deposit in your PayPal account.

She's busy running her business, so if you're late billing her, she's most likely going to be late paying you. A professional invoicing system should be part of your freelance business setup. Every invoice should specify, at a minimum:

- The name of your business
- Payment terms (e.g., due date)
- Product/service for which you're billing
- How charged (e.g., by the hour, by the project)
- Time covered (where applicable)
- Total amount due

Follow Up on Past-Due Invoices

Within a couple of days after the invoice is due, send a reminder to your client. If another day or two passes and you still receive no response, pick up the phone and call. Politely ask if he received your reminder and when you can expect payment. Something along the lines of:

If you're as swamped as I am, I know this may be an oversight, but I'm just calling to see if you got the reminder I sent about invoice number 2047 for the Jane Doe project, which was due almost a week ago.

Don't let your client—or whomever you speak with—off the hook with vague responses. Get specifics and follow up with a short e-mail, which gets what you all agreed upon in the phone conversation in writing:

Thanks for taking my call and making sure that the invoices gets paid by June 7. I really appreciate it. Hope the project goes well, and I look forward to working with you again soon. I know you have the John Doe project coming up. Reach out if I can be of assistance in any way.

Best,
Bob

Many times it truly is an oversight when clients don't pay on time. A slight nudge is all it takes for most to rectify the situation.

What to Do When Clients Don't Pay

Despite your best efforts—calls, e-mails, dropping by their offices unannounced to collect payment (when possible), having an attorney draft a letter threatening to sue—some clients just don't pay.

It can't be stressed enough that this is very rare, and the chances of it happening can be greatly mitigated by doing your upfront due diligence. But if it's been months on end and the client has in effect disappeared or proven that he has no intention of paying, you have a couple of options.

Sic a Collections Agency on Him

When you report a nonpaying client to a collections agency, they will take over your collection efforts, usually for a whopping 30 to 50 percent of the balance they collect. So if you're owed $5,000 and they only collect $3,000, they will keep $900 to $1,500 of this amount.

Still, this can be worth it because it usually doesn't cost you anything upfront; they'll likely be much more aggressive in collecting than you have the time or wherewithal for; and it can show up on the delinquent client's credit report.

Some collection agencies will also outright buy the invoice from you, usually for pennies on the dollar because they're taking a big risk of not getting paid. If you're owed $10,000 they may offer to buy the invoice for 10 percent ($1,000). If they do eventually collect the entire ten grand, they won't owe you anything else. Only you can decide if this is worth it to you.

> **FREELANCER TIP**
>
> If you've gone the legal route and sued the client and won a judgment, as discussed in the following section, a collections agency will usually pay you a higher percentage because a court has already determined that the client owed the debt, and now all they have to do is collect.

Sue in Small-Claims Court

Another option is to file the paperwork for a small-claims court suit, which usually has set limits on the dollar amount you can sue for. Filing is easy; the process is actually designed for the do-it-yourselfer who opts not to hire an attorney.

The hard part is the process itself—the waiting. It can be long and time-consuming, but you have a great chance of winning a judgment against your client if all your paperwork is in order. Then, you have to collect on the judgment, which is a whole other process. If the client lives in another state, you may need to hire an attorney in that state to help you collect, which can be costly.

This is why it's important to vet clients upfront. You'll save yourself a lot of time, money, and grief.

When to Drop Slow Payers

Obviously, you'll drop a client who doesn't pay, but slow payers should be given a hard look too, especially if they consistently take forever to pay.

What's a slow payer? Anyone who pays more than thirty to sixty days past the original due date. The reason you should be concerned about such clients is your cash flow. Cash flow is the difference in amount of cash available at the beginning of a period (aka the opening balance) and the amount at the end of that period (aka the closing balance). If the balance is higher at the end of a period, then the business has positive cash flow; if it's lower, then you have negative cash flow.

If you have $5,000 in outstanding invoices due, and it's time to pay your employees, your rent, and your utilities and you only have $3,000 in the bank, you're going to have cash flow problems. The slow-paying client is in effect strangling the growth of your business.

This is why these types of clients can be as detrimental to your business as nonpaying clients. They keep you in a constant state of anxiety, wondering when—and indeed, if—you're going to get paid.

When you're stressed, it's harder to concentrate. This can cause your work to suffer, which can keep you from attracting better-paying clients, not to mention the time you spend chasing them for payment. You can work yourself into broke-dom with this kind of client.

So while getting paid from slow-paying clients is about the money, it's about more than that. It's about the impact it has on you personally, lost productivity, and the overall impact on your bottom line.

As stated previously, the vast majority of clients are eager to pay. All they want is good value for their money. Vet them well, give them value, and you should have no problems getting paid for your freelance services.

Which Payment Methods to Accept

You can opt to be paid online (e.g., via PayPal), by check, credit card, or by direct deposit into your bank account. Following is an overview of each.

PayPal

This is a widely used way to get paid online. If a company works with freelancers, they most likely know about PayPal. It's free to open a PayPal account.

You don't have to reveal any of your financial information to the client and she doesn't have to reveal any of her information to you. PayPal is the intermediary. This is what makes it such a trusted way to do business on the web.

PayPal has a built-in invoicing system and it's easy to create monthly statements of sales, chargebacks, fees paid/sent, and so on. Come tax time, this is invaluable.

The cost of using an account is 2.9 percent of the transaction plus thirty cents per sale, and you can accept all forms of payment (eCheck, credit cards, and debit cards). There are no hidden fees and you don't have to pay anything until you get paid for selling something.

If tens of thousands of dollars are flowing through your PayPal account, fees can really add up, but you can claim these fees as a business expense on your taxes, so they're not a total loss.

Check

The upside to this payment method is that no fees are deducted. The downside is that it comes via snail mail, and you run the risk of the check being lost in the mail or lost once it gets to you (if you don't use mobile banking). You'll also have to go to the bank to deposit it, then wait for it to clear.

Strangely enough, many of your larger clients will be the ones still tied to paying via this method. It's because they usually do their billing on a set cycle: monthly, quarterly, etc. They have an accounting, finance, and/or billing department that processes all invoices. Many times, their preferred method of payment is still the trusty paper check.

They'll ask you to fill out a W-9 tax form, which is officially known as a Request for Taxpayer Identification Number (TIN) and Certification. You don't have to provide any banking information, and with the new scanning and sending options for depositing checks, this old-school way of getting paid has moved into the twenty-first century.

Direct Deposit

Direct deposit is one of the quickest ways to receive payments. All you have to do is fill out a direct deposit authorization form, which asks for the following information:

- Your name
- Your address
- The number of the account that you want the funds to be deposited into
- Your bank's routing number

Most direct deposit payments clear within two business days. In rare cases, a bank may charge a nominal fee for a direct deposit. In the vast majority of cases, recipients aren't charged a fee. In fact, many banks encourage customers to use direct deposit to avoid unnecessary fees.

Wire Transfers

This option can take a few days to a week to clear, depending on your bank and where the funds are coming from. Domestic wire transfers usually clear within twenty-four business hours; international transfers usually clear in three to five business days.

In order to receive this type of payment, you will have to fill out a wire transfer form, which includes your name and address, your telephone number, your bank account number, and your bank's routing number.

Some banks charge for wire transfers (in the neighborhood of $25); some don't. Again, it depends on the bank, where the funds are coming from and from whom they're coming. This payment option is used mostly by freelancers who can't or don't use PayPal (or their clients don't) and who deal with international customers.

In addition to an incoming wire fee, your bank may charge what's known as an exchange fee (aka currency spread). If your bank uses an intermediary bank, you may be charged a fee for this as well.

An intermediary bank (aka correspondent bank) is a bank that acts on behalf of the beneficiary bank (your bank). Payments come to this bank before being credited to your account, so that's why the bank charges you a fee.

The bottom line on wire transfers: They are a fast, easy, reliable way to get paid, but their costs can mount up.

In the case of wire transfers and direct deposits, make sure that the information you enter on the forms you have to fill out is accurate, especially the routing number and your account number. Otherwise, you risk having funds erroneously deposited into someone else's account. However, most financial institutions have systems in place that prevent payments from being deposited into accounts with a different name. So even if you get your account and/or the routing number wrong, you will most likely be alerted by your bank that something is amiss.

If by some chance you're expecting a direct deposit or wire transfer that hasn't come through, check with your bank to be sure that it has the correct information on file.

Credit Cards

Many of your smaller clients will opt to pay using plastic. Just know, it's one of the more expensive options for getting paid as a freelancer because you normally have to pay a subscription/monthly fee, as well as transaction fees and sometimes even card reader fees.

While apps have cut out or reduced some of these fees, accepting credit cards usually means you have to be face to face with your client to get paid. This is inconvenient in many cases.

FREELANCER TIP

Online merchants like PayPal process credit card payments, so it's kind of redundant to sign up with a credit card merchant to process payments. As you can tell, PayPal is by far the most popular option, especially in the United States, for getting paid as a freelancer.

Invoicing Methods

There are many affordable, easy-to-use invoicing systems on the market, usually as part of some larger bookkeeping system. Here are four popular ones: QuickBooks, FreshBooks, Zoho, and of course, the aforementioned PayPal.

Chapter 10

Kicking It Up a Notch! How to Get Ongoing Clients

Once you get those first few clients under your belt—whether by sheer blind luck, on a wing and some desperate prayers, or by actively following some of the steps outlined in previous chapters—you may be so busy that scaling your freelance business is the last thing on your mind.

But wait a minute there, you hardworking little soul. You don't want to have to work this hard for the rest of your career, do you? This is what scaling your business is all about: replication and efficiency—working smarter instead of harder.

Let's take a closer look at this concept.

What Exactly Does It Mean to "Scale" a Business?

If you ever watch shows like *Shark Tank*, you'll sometimes hear the millionaire and billionaire investors say something along the lines of: "The business isn't scalable. I'm out." Sometimes they'll ask, "How are you going to scale this? I don't see how I'll ever get my money back. I'm out."

What exactly do they mean? What's all this talk about scaling? Scaling can mean different things, depending on context, but here, we're talking about growth. An article in *Fortune* magazine explains, "Businesses that scale are businesses with operating leverage. Put simply, if you add operating costs (sales, marketing, administrators, R&D, etc.) at the same rate you grow revenue, then your business does not scale. Alternatively, if additional revenue requires relatively smaller and smaller additions to operating costs, then congratulations . . . your business scales!"

For example, let's say you start out as a one-person software programming firm. You get busy, so you hire another freelance programmer. Now you can take on more projects, but your earnings don't increase by that much because you're paying your employee the going market rate.

But imagine you start outsourcing jobs to programmers in less-expensive parts of the world where the market rate is much less. This is more possible than ever thanks to technology. You're still paying the going market rate to your employees, but your overhead is much less than if all your employees worked in this country. Hence, profits increase with each new client you bring on.

Congratulations, you're scaling your business!

Service-Oriented versus Product-Oriented Businesses

Scaling service-oriented businesses—the kind many freelancers operate—is more difficult than scaling product-oriented businesses because costs tend to increase at a higher rate along with profits. Product-oriented businesses tend to have a core set of assets that are developed initially. These can then be monetized at a very low marginal cost. Technology is one field where this is very common.

For example, take an applications designer. Once the app has been created, it's all about customer acquisition—that is, getting people to download it. The more customers who download the app, the more money you earn—without having to invest in more software development (at least until it's time to update or tweak the existing app).

See the difference?

The primary difficulty in scaling a service-oriented business is duplicating yourself. To explain, when you start a product-oriented business, the product is what the customer purchases. But when you start a service-oriented business, you—the services you provide—are the "product." So finding others who will care about your business and dispense services with the care and attention to detail that you do can be a hurdle. That's why the biggest expenditure for most businesses—large and small—is investment in employees.

While finding good help can be challenging, it is possible, of course. In fact, many successful freelancers often partner with other independent professionals—either directly, via a formal contractual relationship, or informally, via a referral system whereby leads are passed from one to the other depending on the job at hand. Either way, reaching out to other independent contractors is a smart solution to finding qualified help—and growing your freelance business.

Now that you understand what scaling your freelance business is all about, let's get into the specifics of how to do it.

How to Scale Your Business

There are a bazillion different ways to scale a business. Every freelancer is different, so it all depends on what your objectives are. Following are some basic steps that can scale any business.

Automate

In business, time is money, so anything that you can automate gives you more hours in a workday—which can be used for other things. Remember all those productivity tools discussed in Chapter 8? Look back over that list. What's on there that you can use to wring more hours out of a day?

Take inventory of any tasks that you routinely perform and ask yourself, "Can I automate this? Is it more cost-effective to hire someone to do it for me?"

If the answer is yes, then do it without blinking. You'd be amazed at how spending money upfront can double or triple your earnings—all because you freed up valuable time that you can put to better use.

Remember, as a freelancer time is the most precious resource you have. It's not your clients, it's not your equipment, it's not even your ideas—as fabulous as they may be. Not to sound cruel, but all of these things are replaceable.

Time is not renewable. Once a second, a minute, an hour, a day, a week has passed—there's no getting it back. This is what makes time your most valuable resource. Never forget this—and maximize it whenever possible.

Diversify Offerings

Remember in Chapter 7 when we discussed expanding service offerings? What could be easier than giving existing customers more of what they want to scale a business? So if you start out with one product or service, actively hunt for others that are easy add-ons. For example, if you design and sell custom doghouses (don't laugh, the pet industry is huge!), what are some products that go hand in hand with this?

- Chew toys
- Water bowls
- Personalized flea collars
- Dog clothes
- Leashes

The list is endless. You don't even have to produce these extra add-ons yourself. You can buy them wholesale or use a drop-shipping service to fulfill orders—all while doing what you do best: building doghouses.

It's all about increasing the dollar value of each order, while keeping costs more or less level so that earnings grow by a defined margin over set costs.

Outsource/Delegate

Many freelancers have type A personalities. In some ways, their very makeup is what gives them the courage to step out on their own in the first place. Here are some common traits ascribed to these go-getters:

- Competitive
- Outgoing
- Ambitious
- Impatient
- Proactive
- Aggressive
- Rigidly organized
- Concerned with time management

These are awesome characteristics, just the sort of things that make a freelancer successful. There's a downside though. Many people with these characteristics are control freaks, who have a hard time loosening their control over every aspect of their business. That can interfere with scaling your business if you are unwilling to let go of some control.

Even if you're not a classic type A, you may have some trouble delegating responsibilities to others. But failure to do so can strangle the growth of your freelance business.

Anthony Smith, CEO of Insightly, a customer relationship management (CRM) software, sums up why it can be hard to release control, and why it's important that you do.

Start-up executives frequently try to do everything on their own. However, a CEO's role needs to evolve with his or her company.

If you're spending too much time with marketing, you need to delegate that responsibility. The same goes for hiring or any aspect of managing the business.

When you first start out, it's just you, your ideas, and your way of doing things. It can be hard to change that. But as Smith says, if you don't evolve, neither will your freelance business.

Remember, scaling is about replicating what you do on a larger scale while improving efficiency. In order to grow your freelance business, you're going to have to release control at some point, otherwise your income will be limited to only what you yourself can do. This is a recipe for disaster.

Control Costs

When one company takes over another, what's one of the first things they usually do? Cut costs, right? This may mean firing employees, offering buyouts to others, shutting down certain divisions, or outsourcing to cheaper manufacturers. This is all done to cut costs.

When you start to scale, you need to take the same surgical eye to your business. Following are three common fixed costs you should assess.

1. Supplies/Raw Goods

Can you get your supplies and raw materials cheaper by using a different supplier or by buying in bulk?

2. Help

Can you hire cheaper talent but keep the quality of your product or service the same? You should never sacrifice quality, which can backfire, costing you more in the end. That being said, the best person for the job may not be the one in your proverbial backyard. Maybe there's someone on the other side of the world who can do the job for less money. Same quality. Same dependability. Cheaper cost.

3. Equipment

The flip side to cutting costs is improving efficiency, which may mean investing in better, more expensive equipment. So when it comes to cost, it's not always about cutting; it can mean spending—at least in the short run.

Will spending $9,000 on that new machine allow you to turn jobs around 50 percent quicker? This means you can in essence double your output for a $9,000 investment. If you're clearing an average of $2,500 on each job, your investment has paid for itself—and then some—in just four completed jobs.

This is the way to look at spending money in your freelance business. It's not so much about what it costs upfront, but what it's costing you over time if you *don't* make the investment. Now if you don't have the money, that's one thing. Then rock on the way you are until you do. But you should always have a scaling strategy in place so that you don't get stuck in an underperforming mode of business. What does this mean?

It means you have no idea of how much money you're losing by not investing in things like upgrading your equipment, outsourcing where possible, and negotiating when you buy goods and services.

Many freelancers fall into the trap of doing the same things year in and year out, working themselves to the bone with no measureable increase in earnings. This is not what freelancing is about. Freelancing is a for-profit business. What is the goal of every business? To increase profits year in and year out.

You started freelancing to make a good living, to carve out a nice life for yourself. You're not supposed to suffer and scrimp and barely get by. You deserve better. This is why scaling is so important.

Run Your Numbers

In business, it's all about the numbers. If this is not one of your strong suits, then you need to hire a CPA who can parse them for you. This is a problem too many freelancers don't take time to really learn, especially those who consider themselves "creative types."

Your numbers are the lifeblood of your business. They should drive every decision you make because they tell you everything you need to know about the health of your business.

When you scale, the first thing you need to determine is how you're going to do it. For that, where do you turn? To your numbers, of course! You should know:

- Which products/services account for most of your sales (know exact percentages)
- What products/services need to be cut
- What products/services need to be added
- What are the added costs associated with doing x
- What are the savings associated with not doing y
- Which supply contracts can be renegotiated to save z
- What pricing structure maximizes revenue today

Get out your balance sheets. It's all there—in your numbers.

What to Expect When You Scale

Exciting things can happen when a business starts to grow. Revenues increase, more contractors or employees are hired, expansion opportunities open up, and your freelance business may even be targeted for acquisition by a larger company. Is someone offering you millions of dollars for your business? Is it time to sell?

The possibilities are endless. How do you know what to do?

Jomaree Pinkard, cofounder of Hella Bitters craft cocktail products, summed it up perfectly:

> You have to understand who you are—your team, your capabilities, what you can accomplish—and your brand identity. You need to understand those two dynamics to know what opportunities you can engage in and what you have to say no to.

The One Thing Almost Every Successful Freelancer Does

Many freelancers never maximize the potential of their businesses, because they make so many mistakes. This is understandable. No freelancer is perfect. Every successful freelancer can look back and palm-face himself a few hundred times from all the silly things he did—all because he didn't know what he didn't know.

What is this one thing successful freelancers do that others don't? They take the time to learn how to become entrepreneurs—to think of themselves as business owners, and take the steps necessary to gain the knowledge they need. Unsuccessful freelancers, on the other hand, stay stuck in "I'm just a freelancer" mode.

Eric T. Wagner, a lifelong entrepreneur and contributing writer to Entrepreneur.com and *Forbes*, explains it this way:

> Most struggling entrepreneurs [freelancers] I know fail in this one area more than others: they're focused on the wrong things. Yes— we must get the work done inside our businesses. And yes—it's important to focus on the details. . . . But here's the rub—if you don't focus on the key activities which move your business forward in a strategic way—you're doomed to stagnate. Forever.

Many of the concepts we've discussed thus far—mentally preparing to freelance, scaling and branding a business, fear of success—these are all part of being a full-fledged, I'm-responsible-for-this-company-and-my-success business owner. That means understanding business basics that propel your freelance business to the next level. You must:

- Know how to generate and read profit and loss statements
- Understand who your core customers are
- Know what each product/service is costing you (to the penny)
- Know when to hire help
- Know what your unique selling point is

Compared to all of this, the relatively straightforward objective of landing gigs is the easy part. It's actually making a living that eludes many freelancers. But it doesn't have to be that way.

From day one, treat your freelance business like a newborn baby whom you want to grow up to be strong, healthy, happy, vibrant, and prosperous. As a parent/caregiver how do you accomplish that?

You spend time with it.

You feed it.

You nurture it.

You plan for its future.

You protect it from harm.

Your business requires the same kind of attention to detail. In short, you work on it to move it forward in a strategic way.

You feed it by bringing in projects to keep it going.

You invest in its future by scaling and branding it.

You protect it from harm by doing what's right for it (not over-spending, paying attention to the bottom line, etc.).

Your freelance business is, for all intents and purposes, your baby. It needs all your love, attention, and protection, just like a baby. One day, it may take flight and leave the nest (that is, you could be bought out or go public), but unless and until that happens, it needs you—and you owe it to yourself to be as prepared as you can to handle that responsibility.

Successful freelancers eventually figure this out.

Chapter 11

To Incorporate, or Not

Incorporate?

"I'm a freelance writer. About the most harm I can cause is a spliced comma. I don't need to incorporate, do I?"

Incorporate?

"I design websites. Why would I need to incorporate to do that?"

Incorporate?

"I'm a software programmer. I went out on my own to avoid corporate drudgery. Why would I want to create the very thing I was trying to get away from?"

Are any of these questions running through your head? There are some pros and cons to incorporating. The vast majority depend on the type of freelance business you start, whether or not you have employees, your risk of being sued, the size of your investment in your business, and how comfortable you are with risk.

We'll discuss each of these in a pros and cons section in just a bit, but first, let's examine what it means to incorporate and what type of business structure may be right for your freelance business.

What Does Incorporating Mean?

Although the word *incorporate* may conjure up visions of lawyers and reams of documents and dollars flying out of your pocket, it's actually a pretty simple process. It's one of the things that make America great—practically anyone can start a business, and you can set it up any way you wish with minimal fuss.

To incorporate means to separate yourself as an individual from your business. Following are four common types of business structures. Three of them involve incorporating. The first one—sole proprietorship—is the only one where there is no line of demarcation between you and your business.

Common Business Structures

Sole Proprietorship

According to the Small Business Administration (SBA), more than 70 percent of U.S. businesses are owned and operated by sole proprietors or sole traders. One reason this type of business structure is so popular is because it's so easy.

You don't have to do anything in the way of filing paperwork. You just . . . start your business. Of course, depending on your type of business, you must follow all proper laws when it comes to things like licensing and permits.

A sole proprietorship is an unincorporated business owned and operated by an individual. There is no distinction between the business as an entity and you, the owner. You *are* the business. You're entitled to all the profits generated by the business, and of course, you suffer the financial consequences when and if the business loses money.

Advantages of Being a Sole Proprietor

Cheap and easy to start. As mentioned, you don't have to file any paperwork to be a sole proprietor. As long as everything is in order legally with your licensing and any permits you might need, you're good to go.

Tax preparation. Because there is no legal separation between you and your business, you will continue to file taxes as an individual. You won't be double taxed, once as an individual and once as a corporation. Also tax rates for sole proprietorships are some of the lowest of all business structures.

Freedom from oversight. Unlike corporations where there might be shareholders to account to and specific government regulations to be followed, sole proprietors are relatively unencumbered by restrictions. They can operate as they see fit and are only accountable to themselves.

The Biggest Disadvantage of Being a Sole Proprietor

Personal liability. If someone sues you and wins, everything you own could be at risk. Because there is no legal separation between you and your business as a sole proprietor, you're liable for its financial losses. This includes any losses you incur as a result of employee misdeeds or actions.

Limited Liability Corporation (LLC)

This is essentially a hybrid business structure. It's a corporation in that it separates you as an individual from your business. It gives your business a legal identity that is distinct from you.

It is not a corporation in that it gives you the tax breaks a sole proprietor and/or partnership may enjoy. How? All the profits and losses generated by the business "pass through" the owner's personal tax return. There's no need to file a separate corporate tax return. This, of course, means that you avoid being taxed twice—just as with a sole proprietorship.

FYI, the owners of an LLC are known as "members." Depending on the state, members can be just one individual, or two or more individuals, corporations, or other LLCs.

Advantages of an LLC

Liability. Your assets are protected from any business decisions or actions of the LLC. For example, if your business (the LLC) gets in debt or is sued, your personal assets are usually exempt from any judgments issued against you.

Profit sharing. Corporations can have strict, complex profit-sharing rules; not so with an LLC. As a member, you can distribute profits as you see fit.

Tax preparation. Remember, you don't have to file a separate tax return, which makes filing taxes just slightly more cumbersome than filing as an individual.

Disadvantages of an LLC

Liability. There's a reason it's called a "limited" liability corporation, and that's because you may still be personally liable for some things, for example the LLC's loans. As a member of an LLC, you are not automatically shielded from wrongful acts, including those of any employees or other contractors you may hire.

Self-employment taxes. Unless you elect to be taxed like a corporation, which has a lower tax burden, the profits of the LLC will flow through your personal federal tax return and you will be subject to the self-employment tax. This can be quite hefty, especially when you're not used to paying it.

Just how hefty? It's explained on the Social Security Administration's site for tax year 2015:

> Currently [if you're *not* a freelancer], you and your employer each pay a 6.2 percent Social Security tax on up to $118,500 of your earnings and a 1.45 percent Medicare tax on all earnings. If you're self-employed, you pay the combined employee and employer amount, which is a 12.4 percent Social Security tax on up to $118,500 of your net earnings and a 2.9 percent Medicare tax on your entire net earnings.

If your earned income is more than $200,000 ($250,000 for married couples filing jointly), you must pay 0.9 percent more in Medicare taxes.

Role confusion. Because LLCs are hybrid corporations, they tend not to have defined roles like other corporations, such as directors, managers, and employees.

While this may work just fine when you're the only member, if you decide to seek outside funding, for example, this lackadaisical structure can be a bit confusing for investors—who tend to prefer more concrete roles.

Dissolving. As a sole proprietor, when you no longer want to operate your freelance business, there are no forms to file. Not so with corporations. You have to file forms (articles of dissolution) to formally dissolve the corporation, and depending on the state, you may have to pay a fee.

You also must cancel all licenses and permits associated with the LLC, cancel your EIN and fictitious business name, and notify debtors and creditors that you're dissolving the business. It's not as simple as just closing up shop, as it would be if you were a sole proprietorship.

S Corp/C Corp

Most freelancers who choose to set up a full-blown corporation usually go with an S corp instead of a C corp because of the tax benefits.

The Difference Between an S Corp and a C Corp

A C corporation is, for all intents and purposes, an individual. In fact, the Supreme Court has ruled that corporations are, indeed, "persons." As such, they are subject to taxation.

C corporations must pay their own income tax on profits. The reason they don't make sense as a business structure for the vast majority of freelancers is that this sets up double taxation. You pay a personal income tax when you receive income from this type of corporation, in addition to the corporate tax.

That's why most freelancers who do set up corporations choose S corps. An S corporation is similar to a C corporation, but the way taxes work is different. In an S corp, your income flows through the corporation without being taxed. It is only taxed when it's taken as, personal income. This way, you avoid being double taxed.

S Corp versus Sole Proprietorship

Let's say you don't incorporate at all. You use the common business structure of sole proprietorship, and you earn $60,000 as a freelance translator. But you also move from expensive New York City to the more affordable Jackson, Mississippi, which means your cost of living plummets and you only take a $40,000 salary. You take the other $20,000 in dividends.

If you were a sole proprietor, you would have to pay income tax and self-employment taxes on the whole $60,000. Remember how much those self-employment taxes were? Not exactly peanuts.

As an S corp, you are only liable for income and self-employment taxes on your $40,000 salary. Dividend distributions are not subject to self-employment taxes, which mean you save a lot in taxes.

If you're allergic to numbers and tax laws like a lot of freelancers, your head is probably swimming right now. It can get complicated trying to keep everything straight, which is why you should consult a qualified tax advisor before deciding on a business structure, especially if it's anything beyond sole proprietor.

FREELANCER TIP

Be sure to consult a certified tax professional in your state, as corporation and tax laws vary from jurisdiction to jurisdiction.

Advantages of an S Corp

Tax break. Business income, and all those coveted tax deductions, credits, and losses, are passed through to you as an individual, rather than being taxed as a corporation, which means double taxation. Then there's the tax break on dividend distribution, as discussed previously.

Liability. Your personal assets are protected from the claims of business creditors.

Disadvantages of an S Corp

IRS trigger. Because of the way income can be distributed in this type of corporation, it can trigger more attention from the Internal Revenue Service. For example, the division between salary and dividends must be "reasonable." What's reasonable? Well, that's up to the IRS, and the agency watches these types of payouts very closely and will even recharacterize the income if it determines that the payments were "unreasonable." This could mean higher taxes, and maybe even other penalties and fees.

Strict qualifications. S corps must adhere to some pretty stringent guidelines. For instance, only individuals, certain estates and trusts, and certain tax-exempt organizations can be shareholders. This won't be a stumbling block for most freelancers, but you just have to be a bit more careful that you have all your i's dotted and t's crossed when you select this business structure.

Tax filings. Your taxes are going to be a bit more convoluted than filing as an individual. There are certain schedules that you'll have to fill out.

Expenses. In addition to paying for the forms and the filing fees to set up your S corp, your professional fees will go up, specifically your accounting fees. Most accountants and other professional tax preparers charge more to handle corporate taxes, and even if you decide to go the do-it-yourself route and use a tax preparer like TurboTax, you'll pay more than you would if you were filing an individual tax return.

Dissolving. Just like with a LLC, you have to file paperwork to dissolve the corporation if you decide to close up shop.

Some Overall Pros and Cons to Incorporation

As you can see from the discussion thus far, deciding whether or not to incorporate has implications beyond just deciding on a company structure. It impacts how much you pay in taxes, whether or not your personal assets are protected, and how likely you are to be audited. Following are some common pros and cons of incorporating that can help you decide whether or not it's right for your freelance business.

Con: paperwork. There's paperwork on the front and back ends when you incorporate. When you start you must file the articles of incorporation with your state government. Some states allow you to file online, and others permit you to mail the form to your secretary of state's office. You can also personally deliver your articles of incorporation to the secretary of state's office.

However you do it, it must be done, since failure to ensure receipt of the articles by this state office could cause you to be held personally liable for the actions of the unformed corporation.

On the back end, if you decide to close up shop, you must file corporate dissolution paperwork to officially close the business.

You can find the proper forms on your state's secretary of state or corporations division website. Look for a form named something like certificate of dissolution, certificate of cancellation, or articles of dissolution.

Once you send it in, you're not done. You must then wait for the state to send you a certificate of dissolution or similar document stating that the business has legally been dissolved, which you then file in your corporate or LLC records book.

If you're thinking, "It's just me. I'm a one-person corporation. I don't have to go through all of this, do I?" The answer is a resounding, "Yes, you do!" If you don't file the proper paperwork to dissolve your corporation or LLC, you could face thousands of dollars in fees and penalties in the years ahead. By officially dissolving, you let creditors know that your business can no longer incur business debt. This is important because in some states, if you don't notify creditors and customers that you're closing up shop, they can sue you for a longer period.

So yes, dissolving your corporate entity the right way is the only way to go. It protects you on a myriad of fronts, now—and in the future.

Con: ongoing fees. Most states require corporations to pay ongoing annual fees, which can include franchise tax fees, annual report filing fees, annual registration fees, and annual tax fees. Check with your state's secretary of state or corporations division to determine what fees you're responsible for as a corporation owner.

Pro: financing. One thing you may not give any thought to when you start freelancing is outside financing. In the beginning, you're probably just focused on being able to earn enough to survive and thrive.

But what if your freelance business takes off and you need to hire other freelancers, buy new equipment, or purchase more raw goods to expand production? Then, you may find yourself applying for bank loans or turning to venture capitalists for funding. Many won't even entertain your request unless you're a corporation. If you find yourself facing this situation, it would most likely be a good idea to incorporate.

Pro: acquiring clients. Some prospects consider doing business with individuals too risky. So you could be locking yourself out of potential lucrative deals by not incorporating.

Pro: liability. As discussed previously, one of the biggest advantages to incorporating is your personal assets are protected. As the government considers a corporation to be a legal entity—a person—all profits and losses belong solely to it, not you as the owner.

Five Questions to Help You Decide

The best way to decide if you should incorporate is simply to write it down. So grab a sheet of paper and a pen or pencil, and answer the following questions.

1. What Type of Freelance Business Are You Starting?

For example, if you're a freelance fashion writer, you may decide that it's not worth the bother. But, if you have a freelance bookkeeping business, because you deal with client finances, you may want the added protection of a corporate structure. Also, it presents a more professional image.

2. Will You Have Employees and/or Hire Other Contractors?

Consider this: you contract with another freelancer to help you with a big project from a new client. The client never pays, but you're still on the hook for paying the freelancer you contracted. They sue. Just because you don't have full-time employees does not mean that you are inoculated from being sued.

3. Can You Save Money?

When you incorporate, you can save money because—thanks to the U.S.'s love of all things capitalist—corporations are taxed at a lower rate than individuals.

For example, let's say you're a commercial photographer and decide you want to turn the basement of your house into a full-blown studio. In order to start saving for this, you leave money, say $50,000, in the business instead of taking it as a salary. Because you didn't take this profit as an income distribution, you won't be taxed on it if you are a corporation. How much does that save you? As a sole proprietor, those "retained profits" would be taxed at your individual tax rate—let's say it's 25 percent, or $12,500. As a corporation, that same $50,000 would be taxed at the much lower corporate rate of 15 percent, or $7,500. So as a corporation you save $5,000.

Remember though, corporations are subject to annual fees, and the paperwork and tax preparation is much more cumbersome than filing as a sole proprietor.

Weigh this. On the one hand, you're saving thousands, but what will it cost you in time, stress, and overall aggravation? Again, it's something only you can decide.

4. What's at Risk If You Don't Incorporate?

Do you own a home or have other investments that you stand to lose if someone sues you and wins? Having the shield of some type of business structure between you and your personal assets can provide peace of mind.

Even if you don't have any seizeable assets, a judgment could still hurt you. Your personal credit rating will suffer, and your bank account could be frozen or seized. This could prevent you from conducting business, costing you even more.

5. Are You Comfortable Taking the Risk of Not Incorporating?

When all's said and done, only you can assess your risk level and what you're comfortable with. The key is to make an informed decision.

Legal Advice Every Freelancer Needs to Know

One of the running themes throughout the discussion on whether or not to incorporate has been liability. America is one of the most litigious societies on earth. So yes, as a freelancer you can be sued. People sue for any and everything, and even if a suit is without merit and eventually dismissed, it can still cost you thousands, not to mention lost productivity, stress, and lost income while dealing with the situation.

So, how can you avoid this? It's simple. Buy errors and omissions insurance. The cost is minimal compared to what you will save if you are ever sued. As one freelance web designer who was sued summed up:

> What you're really buying is peace of mind. . . . Litigation is expensive, and the stress of being in a situation you can't control is considerable. The uncertainty and loss of sleep can have a real impact on your life and your workday.
>
> No matter how honorable, loving, and kind you think you are, someone will eventually be upset with you. Be prepared. Have your errors and omissions policy and general liability insurance paid up, and know the name of your insurance agent.

Following are the most common types of business insurance.

Business Liability Insurance

You know how when you rent an apartment and you get renter's insurance in case someone robs you or a ceiling collapses and your belongings are destroyed. Renter's insurance replaces it, right?

Business liability insurance is similar to this. It protects a company and/or business owner in the event of a lawsuit or some other third-party claim. Coverage includes any financial liability incurred, in addition to expenses related to the company's legal fees.

The three common types of business liability insurance are:

- *General liability insurance:* This protects any assets your freelance business has and covers any costs you may incur as a result of accidents or property damages or injuries caused by you or your employees.
- *Product liability insurance:* This insurance is for product-oriented businesses. Product liability insurance shields against claims of

personal injury or property damage that may be caused by any products sold or supplied by your business. It pays legal fees and other suit-related court costs.

- *Professional liability insurance (PLI):* This insurance, also known as professional indemnity insurance (PII) and as errors and omissions (E&O) insurance, helps protect professional advice- and service-providing individuals and companies (for instance, financial planners) from negligence claims and any damages that may be awarded in a civil suit.

FREELANCER TIP

Errors and omissions insurance kicks in when a client sues you for negligence or some other perceived mistake that caused financial loss or damage. This form of insurance covers hiring an attorney to defend your case in court and any settlements, fees, or judgments for which you may be found liable.

The cost of E&O insurance depends on a number of factors, including but not limited to: your business's location, number of employees, type of business you operate, and annual revenue.

Covering Yourself

Whether or not you decide to incorporate, the one thing that you should consider is how to cover yourself in case you are ever sued, especially as in the United States, creditor judgments assessed against you can potentially become permanent. What this means is, if you're sued today and lose, your assets could be vulnerable for the rest of your life. Yes, that long!

The length of a judgment depends on the laws of your state, and the method the creditor uses to try and collect. In some states, it is effective between five and seven years. In other states, for example New York, it can last for twenty years or more.

Before you make any decisions, consult an attorney and a small business expert. Why these two professionals? An attorney is trained to think in terms of what would happen if you don't incorporate, so she may lean toward incorporating.

An experienced businessperson, for example, a member of SCORE at your local SBA or a fellow small business owner at a chamber of commerce who's been in business for years, may be able to give you a different perspective. They may advise against incorporating and suggest just picking up E&O insurance.

The final decision is yours—but at least you will have made it armed with facts instead of conjecture.

Chapter 12

Common Freelance Pitfalls to Avoid

Because freelancing is one of those dream careers that many aspire to, it comes with its share of scams—as with any other often-sought-after dream. Some scams are designed to take your money, others are designed to get work from you for free, and yet others aim to steal your very identity. Here is a list of some of the most common scams, and how to avoid them.

The Scams Pitfall

Scamming freelancers, sadly, can be uncommonly easy because so many are new, eager to work, and want to build their portfolios. But if something smells like a rat—even if it looks like a lobster dripping in butter and gets all your creative juices flowing—it's a rat. That feeling in the pit of your stomach, no matter how small, is the voice in the basement yelling at you that this is a scam. Heed it! Chances are very, very small that you're passing up a legitimate opportunity.

The "Samples" Scam

One of the most common scams pulled on freelancers is the "samples" scam. It works like this. Let's say you're a freelance online writer. You'll be contacted about a job—usually a pretty large one. In this case, let's say it's for $2,000. The company wants ten articles of 750 words each about spring bridal trends. The job needs to be completed within three days.

In order to apply though, you need to send a writing sample—an original one—on a topic they select. If your sample is good enough, they'll give you the job. Oh, and by the way, they're not paying you for the sample they're requiring.

You get excited. Wow, two grand on the table! Ten articles of only 750 words on spring bridal trends. You've been a bridesmaid a gazillion times. Your sister just got married four months ago and you helped her plan her whole wedding, including selecting the bridal party wear. You love brides. You want to be a bride. Your whole wedding is planned out in your head!

You could write on this in your sleep. Of course they're going to love your writing sample. This job is as good as yours!

Hold on there. You are most likely being scammed. How can you tell?

Writing for Free

Most legitimate companies will pay you for an *original* writing sample. If they contact you directly, it's usually because they've visited your site or seen samples of your work elsewhere and like what they saw. If you don't have a sample on the topic they want you to write on, prospects will ask for simple samples or will commission an original sample from you, one they're perfectly willing to pay for.

Scammers get free content and work by pulling the "samples" scam. They contact lots of freelancers with the same offer. Imagine if someone's launching a new website about bridal fashion. She contacts 100 freelance writers, and thirty-five of them fall for the writing sample scam. That's thirty-five free pieces of content she's gotten. She tells all of the thirty-five freelancer writers that their samples aren't good enough, or she says she's awarded the job to someone else.

If you're one of the thirty-five, you're probably bummed, but you don't think anything more about it. Until while web surfing one day you find your original article on the site—the one they said wasn't good enough, or that they'd hired someone else to write. The site's owner has successfully scammed you into writing for her for free.

Signs of a "Samples" Scam

Scams show warning signs to the alert. After you've been in the freelance business for a while, you learn to recognize these signs almost instinctively. The "samples" scam has a few classic signs:

- Usually it contains the promise of a large order
- The deadline is tight
- The prospect wants original work for free
- He wants you to get started right away
- He balks at any form of upfront payment

Ask prospects like this how they heard about you. After all, if they want you to do a big job, isn't it strange that they want you—a virtual stranger—to start so quickly? Don't they have someone in their referral network they could give the work to?

Even if the prospect passes this part of the smell test, if he asks for a free sample or wants you to get started immediately with no upfront payment and no contract, this is a big red flag.

Think about it this way: If you were going to pay someone thousands of dollars for a job, wouldn't you want a contract in place. If you've vetted the freelancer properly and are sure she's the right person for the job, wouldn't you understand that she expects an upfront payment?

Scammers always try to operate outside of the lines. On some level, their approach doesn't seem legitimate—you will feel this in your gut. But because you're new, you try to talk yourself into ignoring it because you want the job so badly. Don't.

There are other scams similar to the samples scam that target free-lancers. They include the membership scam, the work-for-low-pay scam, and the revenue-sharing scam. What all of these scams have in common is that you work for free. Following is a summary of each.

Membership scam. You're asked to sign up for some type of monthly recurring membership that is automatically charged to your credit/debit card. A promise of ongoing job leads and/or insider bidding on jobs is usually the enticement. The problem is, the jobs are usually ones you can find yourself on sites such as Craigslist, or any other freelance job listing site. Also the jobs that are sent are either so low-paying and/or outside the scope of your interests and skill set that they're worthless. It can be practically impossible to cancel your membership. So beware of sites that charge any kind of membership fees for job leads. The best freelance jobs are the ones you track down yourself or that come from reputable, well-known sites.

Work-for-low-pay scam. This scam lures you in with the possibility of ongoing, higher-paying work—if you can prove that you can do the job. The scammer asks you to do something for free, or at a ridiculously low rate, to prove that you can do the job. Then, if you complete the job to his satisfaction, you will be hired and paid a higher, industry-standard rate.

The scam is, they're doing this with tons of other freelancers. No one is being "approved." All the work that's being completed is being done for free or for the low rate advertised.

If you run across a job ad that asks you to do work for free or a ridiculously low rate, with the promise or suggestion of more work will follow if you prove worthy, take a pass. It's most likely a freelance job scam.

Legitimate clients will either accept your already prepared samples as proof that you can do a job or will pay you the normal, industry-standard rate if they want you to do a sample/test job. They won't expect you to work for free.

Revenue-sharing scam. To be clear—not all revenue-sharing jobs are scams. Many reputable companies, such as www.Examiner.com

and www.eHow.com, offer this form of compensation. That being said, most of these types of jobs are not worth it for freelancers—not if you want to earn any real money. Here is how they work: You sign up to provide a product or service, for instance writing articles in a defined niche. You are paid based on the number of views that article receives. For example, you may be paid one cent per click and have to earn a minimum of $25 per month in order to collect payment. This means 2,500 web surfers would have to click on your article in order for you to reach the $25 milestone payout threshold.

Now, if you're writing in a hot niche like entertainment, and 100,000 people click on your article, that's great; you'd earn $1,000. But many freelancers never develop this type of readership, making writing for a revenue-sharing website worthless from a monetary standpoint.

The site usually also retains ownership of the content, which means if you stop writing for them, you can't take it with you and you aren't paid for future clicks. Furthermore, if you never reach the payout threshold, you may never get paid. This means the site, in essence, gets free work from freelancers.

In short, even when the terms are clearly specified upfront, what many revenue-sharing sites amount to is a scam for freelancers. Any job you take on should have clearly defined "cash for service/product rendered" value, not be based on ad clicks or page views.

The Identification Theft Scam

Sites such as Fiverr, Guru, Freelancer, and Upwork are legitimate sites on which freelancers hawk their services. Scammers though, use them for nefarious purposes. So you have to be careful, even though you're working within a legitimate freelance portal.

Here's how the ID scam works.

The client says she wants to hire you for a job. However, instead of paying through the system the freelancing site has set up, she says they want to pay you via direct transfer to avoid fees, so she asks for some personal details.

"Great," you may be thinking. You'll avoid fees too, and the money will be deposited right into your account. What could be more convenient?

Hold on. All those personal details you provide will be used to steal your identity. One day you'll insert your ATM card only to find that the money you did have in the account is gone.

How can you tell someone is working this kind of scam? Well, they're working around the site's system and are asking for personal information. It's unethical to ask for contact info outside of whatever system you're working with. These sites have safeguards in place to protect you

FREELANCER TIP

Avoiding scams is one reason why it pays to vet clients thoroughly, as discussed in Chapter 9. If there's even the tiniest feeling in your gut that something just isn't right, turn down the job. Nine times out of ten, you'll be dodging the proverbial bullet.

What to Do If You Suspect an ID Theft Scam

If someone contacts you via your website, for example, offering to pay upfront through a direct bank transfer, your hackles should immediately go up. Any stranger requesting personal details about you should raise your suspicion; yes, that applies even when they're offering to give you money upfront for a job. That money is the hook that convinces so many to fall for these types of scams.

Instead of providing personal info so that a bank-to-bank transfer can take place, offer an alternative payment option such as PayPal, Authorize.Net, Google Wallet, or 2Checkout. These are safe, secure online payment processors that don't require you to provide personal details to the paying party.

If they refuse this option, red flags should be sprouting faster than tulips in the spring. But if you forge ahead, you can go with the old "send me a check in the mail" option. If the prospect refuses this option, run, run, run. Fast.

Think about it this way: If a stranger came to your door and said he's willing to give you $1,000 if you just give him some personal financial information, would you do it? Probably not, right? You'd look at him as if he had two heads, slam the door in his face, and probably call the police. People who approach you on the Internet are like the stranger on your doorstep. Treat them in the same manner.

"But," you may be thinking, "bank transfers do happen. Lots of businesses pay via bank transfer."

It's true. But especially in the United States you only need to provide limited information for this to happen (usually your bank's routing number and your checking account number). Other information such as your Social Security number, bank account PIN number, credit card number, and your mother's maiden name and birth date are never required.

How to Spot a Legitimate Bank Transfer (ACH) Request

First, note that this is an extremely rare form of payment. Many legitimate companies use online payment processors like PayPal because they don't want your personal information. This protects them too because if their servers are ever hacked and they have all your data, it opens them up to lawsuits. It's why companies like Pay-Pal grew so fast—businesses were eager to escape this type of financial liability.

Only accept this form of payment from a company you've vetted well. Usually, it'll provide you with a form—on company letterhead—to fill out to process payment.

It will ask for your name, address, bank name, account number, and routing number. Sometimes, it'll ask for your e-mail address. That's it. That's all that's needed to complete an Automated Clearing House (ACH) transfer.

One final thing: *Never* click on a link in an e-mail that asks you for personal information to download a form or to be sent to another site. *Ever.* It could be loaded with malware to infect your system at best, and steal your identity at worst. To avoid financial scams, always go to the site itself. Even if you bank online, are used to getting your statements via e-mail, and are 100 percent sure that the e-mail is from your bank, don't click on the link in the e-mail.

Always open a browser window yourself, or click through to your bank from a favorite site you've saved on your device. If you're tired and bleary-eyed from a project, it's easy to mistake a spoof e-mail from them as one from your bank, and click through.

Once you do, they have your log-in information and in a nanosecond, your account can be cleaned out. You will rarely, if ever, recover those funds, especially if they've been stolen from your bank account—as opposed to a credit card, for example.

To learn more about how to stay safe when conducting business online, visit the Consumer Financial Protection Bureau at www .consumerfinance.gov. They offer letters, bulletins, and other materials on a variety of topics, including how to protect yourself and your assets when conducting business online.

Report Scammers

One more thing: Report any scammer you encounter through a work site to the site's administrators. You will be helping to protect other freelancers from the very same scam because you can bet if a scammer has contacted you, they've contacted others as well.

The Pricing Pitfall

Pricing is the one thing that scares the bejesus out of most freelancers. They usually wind up pricing too low because the fear is, "Nobody will hire me at this rate." To you, $75 per hour sounds ridiculous. How can you ever convince somebody to pay you that?

But, do you remember the cost of self-employment taxes? Do you remember how much healthcare is going to cost you? Do you remember those annual corporation fees you're now responsible for and the rise in your accounting fees because your business is a person and your taxes are more complicated? Do you remember the E&O insurance you have to pay for in case some disgruntled nutjob sues you and puts your life's work at risk?

Now are you starting to feel like you deserve that $75 per hour?

If you're thinking, "I ought to be charging a helluva lot more than that!"—that's the spirit. Many freelancers make the mistake of comparing apples (their old salary) to oranges (what they need to charge to really replace that old salary) when they set their rates.

As detailed in Chapter 3, a big part of a full-time employee's salary is comprised of benefits such as paid leave, retirement and savings, and health insurance.

When you set your rates, take this into consideration. For example, if your goal is to replace your $40,000 per year salary from private industry in your first year as a freelancer and you were working in the private industry, you'll really need to earn $56,800 as a freelancer (adding on an additional $16,800—42 percent—to account for the benefits portion of your previous salary).

As you can see, a $40,000 salary with benefits in the corporate world is not the same as a $40,000 salary in the freelance world.

Never forget this when you're setting your rates.

The Confidence Pitfall

You've managed to push through all your freelance fears. You're open for business. You may have even completed a project or two—one you got from a previous boss or from an old college pal. It's friendly territory. They know you, like you, and trust you to do a good job.

Now that chamber of commerce networking you've been doing is paying off. You got a gig from that hotshot marketing firm downtown. If you do a good job, there could be much more work coming your way.

This is when an attack of the nerves can set in. Your confidence is rattled. "Can I really do this?" you wonder. "Is my work really good enough?"

You peek at a client's site again and again. The design is so sleek. The copy is so good. They have case studies from noted professionals there. Why in the world do they want to work with you, a veritable nobody in their high-tech, venture-capital-lavished world?

You want your mommy!

Now it's time to call on that new yoga training. What was that friggin' chant? You break into "Oms" and start breathing as if your life depended on it.

Now it's time to focus on what this really is. Remember in Chapter 1 when we talked about fear of success? What you're feeling now is probably a manifestation of it, or its first cousin, fear of failure.

Either way, trust that it probably has nothing to do with your inability to deliver. After all, this company has probably done its due diligence on you. You've more than likely given them samples; they've viewed your website; and they even agreed to your "they'll never pay this but I'm gonna ask anyway" rate because they believe that you can deliver, that you are capable, and that you're the right fit for the job.

You've done everything right, including getting them to pony up cold, hard cash. That's 90 percent of the battle. Everything you've done to date has led to this moment.

Remember when you slaved over what your unique selling point should be?

Remember when you sent your logo back to the designer five different times to get it just right?

Remember when you ran a dozen different slogans by twenty different friends and family members, bugging them for feedback so much so that they begged you to just pick one and get on with it?

Remember when you slaved over your marketing plan, spending weeks digging into stats about your niche market so that you could effectively deliver what they needed?

Now all that work is paying off. Don't let a momentary dip in your confidence take all that hard work away from you. You're ready. You're prepared. You *can* do this.

The Friends and Family Pitfall

While many of your friends and family will be happy and excited for you, there will inevitably be a few who give you that look as if you're crazy or say something snide like, "Are you sure this is a good idea? Make sure you don't burn any bridges because you might need your job back in six months."

You expect reactions and comments like this from acquaintances and people you know don't like you. It can be a shock when it comes from friends and family—people who are supposed to love you and support your dreams. It's especially painful when you've told them that it's not a whim and that you've given it a lot of thought and have a defined plan of action.

Be careful of people like this. Yes, they're friends, they're family—but they're also confidence drainers and dream snatchers. Many times, this type of reaction springs from their own insecurities, jealousies, and secret desires. They want to have the courage to do what you're doing but they don't, so they tear you down. Most of the time it is not even overtly intentional on their part; they can't help themselves.

When it happens, don't hesitate to let them know how their words and actions make you feel, and ask them to stop. If they don't, take measures to limit your contact with them, especially if every time you see them they denigrate your decision to freelance, or take swipes at how you're doing. "How's that freelance thing working out for ya? Missing that regular paycheck yet?"

You don't need this type of negativity, especially when things may indeed be a little slow and you are already doubting your decision.

You don't want yes people who'll say just what you want to hear. They can be as bad as the naysayers. But you do want a "you can do it" contingent in your corner, people you can turn to to voice your fears and who will encourage you and help you when possible.

The bottom line: surround yourself with people who are supportive, and recognize that sometimes these might not be friends and family.

The Competition Pitfall

You log on, look at your website, and glow with happiness at how well it came out. That web designer you found on that online forum did a great job, especially on your limited budget.

There's just one more thing you need to add to your neat little site. Your biography. You smile and take a sip of coffee. Hmm, your favorite blend. Sometimes you get it just right. That's a good sign; when the coffee comes out perfect, you know it's gonna be a good day.

"Hmm, I've heard that my bio should be more of a professional profile instead of a resume. Let me see how some of my competitors handled this."

You click on the first site. You put your coffee cup down.

Two hours later, your unfinished coffee sits cold, untouched but for that first, delicious sip.

You go back to your little corner of the web. It looked so good two hours ago. Now, after going through a dozen competitor sites, all you can see is what's wrong with yours, how much of your business plan you need to readjust, and what services you need to add. But you have no clue of how to do any of that.

It's too early for a cocktail . . . isn't it?

Maybe retail therapy will handle it. You grab your purse and out the door you go. What started out as a potentially very productive day—remember, you just had one more thing to add to your website— winded up being totally wasted. You spent money you didn't need to spend and got nothing accomplished for your freelancing business.

The Lesson

Looking at the competition is great, but only to help you. Never let the competition drag your down. Aspire to be them one day, whether in sales, in customer acquisition, in customer retention, or in services you offer. But also use them to inspire you to be different, to forge new paths, to make your mark, to be you.

There will always be others you perceive as better—and they may indeed be better. But don't let it stop your flow, dent your confidence, and shift your mindset into one of fear and negativity.

Always let the competition be your guiding light—on the road to success.

The Procrastination Pitfall

As we said back in Chapter 9 when talking about how to meet and beat deadlines, "Procrastination can literally make or break your freelance career. It's a habit you cannot afford." It's a dream snatcher.

What's time when you freelance? Money. So you are literally robbing yourself when you procrastinate.

Kick the Crap Out of Procrastination

Here are five tips for beating procrastination. If you start your freelance career by making these a habit, sure, you may still get robbed of time (hello, Facebook is not going anywhere), but the thief's take won't be so large.

1. Delay Getting Online

Internet surfing is one of the greatest wastes of times in the modern world. You log on to "just check e-mail," and three hours later, you're surfing, reading about the latest sports game, celebrity breakup, and political scandal.

Don't! Unless it's absolutely necessary to log on for your workday, delay it for as long as possible.

2. Time-Block Your Days

We talked about this in Chapter 8. Follow the ICE plan. At the end of every workday, make it a habit to time-block the coming day. That way, you can avoid having to log on first thing the next day. Time-blocking keeps you focused because at every moment of every day, you'll know exactly what you should be doing.

3. Use Automation Tools

One of the things that many people spend time on online is social media. You may log on for a legitimate reason—to update your social media accounts, for example—but before you know it, you've wasted two hours, and only fifteen minutes of that time was spent actually updating your accounts.

Using automation tools like Hootsuite to preschedule posts will make it unnecessary for you to log on at all every day. You can schedule up to a year's worth of posts at one time with tools like this.

You want to engage with your communities on social media, but it doesn't have to be every hour of every day, or every day for that matter. That sort of thing can keep you from more important tasks, usually those you don't like doing, such as cold-calling and getting your tokus to that chamber of commerce meeting. However, those tasks can bring in business immediately.

4. Visualize

This is a Zen-like practice that many reject as impractical. However, visualizing what it will mean to your life to finish what you need to get done today can have a huge impact on how you use your time.

Where do you want to be in a year? Three years? Five? Keeping this vision front and center can help you stay focused.

5. Recognize and Refocus

Inevitably the time thief will snag you in its trap. It gets the best of everyone at some point or other. But, that doesn't mean you have to stay trapped. When you recognize that you're surfing endlessly or have been on social media for too long, stop it. Immediately. Then reboot and refocus.

FREELANCER TIP

Create a vision board—a physical one. Put it in a place where you can see it every day. It's a physical reminder of why you do what you do and there's power in that. Consider this comment from an article by Elizabeth Rider in the *Huffington Post*:

> When you create a vision board and place it in a space where you see it often, you essentially end up doing short visualization exercises throughout the day.
>
> Visualization is one of the most powerful mind exercises you can do. According to the popular book *The Secret*, "The law of attraction is forming your entire life experience and it is doing that through your thoughts. When you are visualizing, you are emitting a powerful frequency out into the Universe." Whether you believe that or not, we know that visualization works. Olympic athletes have been using it for decades to improve performance.

Freelance writer Bev Gray spoke to the power of procrastination. It's a firsthand account of just how bad it can get—and a reminder not to let its grip hold you for too long.

"The Power of Procrastination"
by Bev Gray

Procrastination is a ferocious and dangerous force. Sometimes it pulls you in and you don't even know it happened.

I for one, am a master procrastinator. Enlightened in the art of dawdling. I can faff about with the best of the best. I can make a plethora of different things, but the best thing I make is excuses.

If there were classes in procrastination, I could teach them. If there were awards for wasting time, I could have a mantel chock-full of trophies. I sometimes wish I had a seatbelt on my computer chair that only unlocked after I have written a designated amount of time. But it wouldn't matter, I would find ways to faff about while strapped to a chair. Probably mindlessly wheeling my chair around the house. Why? Because I am a sage shaman at lolly-gagging.

I dally daily without even realizing it. Because if someone asked me, "What are you doing?" I wouldn't respond with the truth, procrastinating. I'd say something that doesn't sound remotely like loafing. I'd say things like cooking, shopping, running, swimming, paddle boarding, googling, organizing a cabinet, walking the dog, changing my air filters, checking social media, watching a funny video of a stranger's baby, etc.

Take now for instance. This moment in time right now. I am procrastinating. I'm supposed to be writing a screenplay, but instead I am writing this article. Why? Because I'm a writer and a procrastinator, and when you have found a way to procrastinate while writing, then you are officially on the road to being a writer. Instead of taking a break from writing by not writing at all, just write something else. . . .

This is the best time in history to be a writer. You can write all lower case. YOU CAN WRITE ALL UPPERCASE. You can use weird fonts. Or . . . . excessive, extreme, punctuation!!!!!! or no punctuation at all.

When I started doing stand-up, I asked an experienced comedian how he came up with jokes. He said, "I keep a pen and notepad on me at all times. Always. I write down every funny thought I have. Most of them get tossed, but some I keep and develop. But you have to start with writing them down. Every day."

So write. Every day. About everything. Or nothing.

Write on your iPhone. Write on your laptop. Write on your iPad. Write in a notebook. Write on a grocery store receipt. Write with pens that make you happy. Write with pens that make you cuss and shake them. Write by telling Siri what you want to say. Write early in the day, write late at night, write during lunch. Write things that rhyme. But not all the time. Write things that make you laugh, or about your greatest gaff. Write things that are forlorn. Write about Little Bighorn.

Get the thoughts out of your head and into written form. Otherwise you are not a writer, you are an idea haver. And we all have ideas. Even dogs and cats have ideas, they just can't write them down . . . but you can.

Now, stop dallying about. Do you want to be a famous reader? Or do you want to be a famous writer?

The Transitioning Pitfall

Sometimes after freelancing for a while, you realize that the niche you've targeted is not right. This could be for a myriad of reasons—it's too small; it's hard to find well-paying clients; or you just don't like it.

As you've been freelancing for a while, you can't imagine going back to a nine-to-five job, so you decide to switch niches. There is one thing you must keep in mind—it can be like starting over.

The reason that choosing a niche is so effective when you freelance is because you get to know a targeted group and their problems intimately. You build your marketing around it, and you pour all your resources and energy into it. When you decide to switch niches, you're going to have to do this all over again: researching, asking questions, putting together a solution that addresses their pain points—in short, build a business around them.

If you're targeting a complementary niche, it will be easier to make the transition, but you should still take the following steps.

Write a New Business Plan

Targeting a different niche means getting your messaging right. So whether your existing one has to be tweaked to penetrate a complementary market or you have to craft a new message altogether, you should do a business plan first.

Skills Assessment Test

When you freelance, you learn a lot. You probably have skills at your disposal that you don't even realize you've picked up that can help you with your transition, so take stock of your existing skills. What have you learned that could make your transition easier?

FREELANCER TIP

Don't forget to take note of your soft skills, including critical thinking, negotiation, adaptability, and communication. These are every bit as important as the more easily identifiable hard skills.

Get That Emergency Fund Ready

What do you do when you're driving and need to make a turn? You usually stop, look to see if anything is coming, slowly make the turn, then press on the gas, right? Making a transition is kind of like this. It takes more time, thought, and energy than it does to keep moving straight, especially when you've picked up some momentum.

The point? As you make the transition, it's going to take some time to build up speed. Your income will likely take a hit, so just as you did before you quit your nine-to-five job to freelance full-time, beef up that emergency fund.

As an aside, you should always have enough in your emergency fund to cover a defined period; three months should be a rock-bottom minimum. Remember to take into account your defined expenses, as discussed in Chapter 4.

Also remember to reassess what's in your emergency fund when life circumstances dictate a big change such as the birth of a child, marriage, or a major purchase such as a car or home.

Keep Old Clients Happy

Until you make the transition complete, your current clients are akin to the security of your old full-time job. So keep them happy. Even though you may be going in a completely different direction, you never know where your next dollar is coming from.

Like your old employer, your old clients can be your biggest source of revenue as you move forward in your newly chosen path, either as continuing clients, or as fertile sources of referral for new clients.

Realize It's Going to Take Time

There will be days where you doubt if you've made the right move when you transition. If you gave it the same careful thought and attention to detail as when you left your full-time job, it most likely is. So be patient with yourself.

Remember, you made the transition from full-time to freelance. You know how to make money under your own steam. You know how to forage for your dinner, and bring it home, clean it, and cook it. Most only know how to buy packaged, or order takeout. You know how to take it from the earth to the pan. You freelance! That's the scariest leap of all for many. Now that you're already on the road, you can most certainly make the turn to go in another direction.

Embrace Change

The definition of transition is "the process or period of changing from one state or condition to another."

Change. It can be scary, whether you're transitioning from a full-time job or from one freelance niche to another. Most often, fear of the unknown is what is most scary. By creating a solid plan, change becomes less of a fear, and more of an opportunity.

Or to paraphrase the Tim Robbins character in the movie *The Shawshank Redemption*, "Do you want to get busy living, or stay busy . . . accomplishing nothing."

Chapter 13

Medical Insurance for Freelancers

Did you know that not having health insurance can lead to a lawsuit?

Imagine you're a freelance translator. You have a contract with a client who is launching his brand in German. Your job is to make sure that all the copy is translated from English to German. The translated copy is due in two days. The client's built his whole marketing campaign around the website going live in three days. He's bought ads on social media, done press releases, done blog tours—all to build anticipation for his online opening in three days.

You fall ill. You can't afford to go to the doctor because you don't have health insurance. Even if you did, you couldn't afford any prescriptions the doctor might write. You try to tough it out and finish the project, but you just can't do it. The flu that's been going around knocks you for a loop for a week. You miss the deadline—costing your client thousands of marketing dollars.

He sues—and wins.

Many freelancers never think of the importance of health insurance. While your overall health and well-being is the most important thing, lack of health insurance can also cause you irreparable financial harm.

Following are seven options for acquiring health insurance as a freelancer.

1. The Affordable Care Act (ACA aka "Obamacare")

As a newly minted freelancer, this is probably the first place you're going to look for insurance. Passage of the ACA in 2010 made health insurance a mandatory purchase for all Americans, and the penalties for not getting it are significant.

Penalties for Not Getting Insured

Here's what an article from Vista Health Solutions has to say on skipping your health insurance:

In 2015 that fine increases to $325 per adult and $162.50 per child or 2 percent of your income, whichever is greater. For 2016 the penalty increases again to $695 per adult and $347.50 per child or 2.5 percent of your income.

Starting in 2017 the Shared Responsibility Payment will still continue to increase, but it will do so according to the current rate of inflation, with the children's penalty being equal to half of the adult penalty, and the total cost of the penalty not to exceed 2.5 percent of a person's annual income.

What You Need to Know about the ACA

The ACA is a complicated piece of legislation, but there are some specifics in it that you need to be aware of.

1. Guaranteed acceptance: Even with a pre-existing medical condition, you can't be denied healthcare coverage.
2. You can stay on your parent's plan until you're twenty-six: This is true even if you no longer live with your parents, are not a dependent on a parent's tax return, or are no longer a student. The policy providing access for young adults applies to both married and unmarried children.

3. There are specified times during the year when you can enroll: For 2016, the open enrollment period was November 1, 2015 to January 31, 2016. You qualify for a special enrollment period, which allows you to enroll outside of the open enrollment timeframe if certain life events happen, such as marriage, having a baby, or you lose existing coverage. If you qualify, you can apply for Medicaid or Children's Health Insurance Program (CHIP) at any time of the year.

4. There are tiered pricing plans to accommodate various budgets: To find out how much you'll pay, once you log onto the site, you'll be asked a series of questions: age, income, number of dependents, zip code, and expected medical use. Expected medical use is how much use you expect to make of doctor visits, lab and diagnostic testing, prescription drug use, and other medical costs for the year. You can choose low, medium, or high. After you plug in all of this information and hit enter, you will be taken to "the marketplace." This shows you which healthcare plans are available in your area, and the specifics of each: deductible, annual and monthly cost, and copayment amounts.

5. The older you are the more it costs: Even if you're still healthy and have low expected medical use, you'll pay more as a fifty-year-old than you will as a thirty-year-old.

6. Your freelance business structure is important: Under the ACA, small businesses with less than fifty employees can offer Small Business Health Options Program (SHOP) plans to their employees, starting any month of the year. While this may not seem like a big deal, it can be important as you grow because in some states sole proprietors are not considered small business owners with regard to health insurance, making them ineligible for SHOP discounts.

7. You can mitigate costs with a subsidy: The ACA includes government subsidies and tax credits to help those who qualify pay for health insurance. The Kaiser Family Foundation created

a nifty little healthcare subsidy calculator (http://kff.org/interactive/subsidy-calculator) that allows you to quickly figure out how much of a subsidy you may qualify for. It will also tell you the most you have to pay for plans within your budget, how much that plan would cost you without the subsidy, what your out-of-pocket costs will be for certain plans, and other coverage options you may want to consider.

Catastrophic Health Insurance

If cost is an issue, at the very least you should consider catastrophic health insurance, which is available under the ACA. Appropriately referred to as "major medical," it covers major life emergencies such as surgery, extended hospital stays, and accidents.

To qualify for this type of plan under the ACA, you must be under thirty or request a hardship exemption, which means that you can't afford insurance in the marketplace.

These plans are designed as short-term safety nets for those who can't afford high monthly premiums. Under the ACA, your catastrophic plan will cover three annual primary care visits and preventive services for free. This includes disease screenings and vaccinations. All other medical expenses are paid out of pocket.

The deductibles are usually high. Under the ACA you will pay more than 40 percent of costs for the cheapest package (the bronze plan), and the deductible is currently $6,850 for a single person, but your monthly premiums are lower than other types of plans. Although the deductible is high, it is good insurance to have in case of an emergency. Who might this be a good option for?

- Young, relatively healthy freelancers who have some savings socked away that can cover the deductible in case an emergency comes up
- Those who can't afford high monthly premiums
- Those who expect to be able to upgrade to a more robust health plan within six months to a year; for example, if you're planning

to get married in three months and your spouse has excellent coverage at her job

2. COBRA (Consolidated Omnibus Budget Reconciliation Act)

If you're coming to freelancing from a full-time job and haven't lined up another healthcare option yet, COBRA might be the best way to go until you can figure out what plan is right for you.

Check with whoever is responsible for handling employee benefits at your company for detailed information. But basically—whether you quit or were fired (unless it was for gross misconduct)—you can keep your company insurance for eighteen months.

When you give your official notice, or are officially notified that you are being let go, it's your employer's responsibility to notify the insurer for you. Then, within fourteen days, the benefits administrator should contact you and ask if you want to sign up for COBRA. You have up to sixty days to decide if you want to enroll.

The downside to COBRA is that while you are entitled to the same benefits, you'll have to pay more for them—usually quite a bit more than when you were with your employer. The reason is, your insurance provider can charge you up to 102 percent of the cost of the plan, and even more if you opt to take the disability provisions as well.

So don't be surprised at the rate, and get busy investigating other suitable options if it's too rich for your new, looking-for-savings-at-all-costs freelance blood.

3. Medicaid

The ACA expanded the scope of Medicaid, making it a viable health-care option for freelancers in some states. Why only some states?

Before the ACA, Medicaid was only available to those with an income up to or below the federal poverty level (FPL). ACA provisions expanded that, allowing those with an income of up to 138 percent of the FPL to take advantage of the program. Another huge change, especially for freelancers, is the allowance of coverage for single, childless adults.

However, not all states accepted these changes in their Medicaid programs. In 2012, the Supreme Court changed the rules, allowing state governors and lawmakers to opt out of widening their Medicaid coverage by including the ACA's changes.

The bottom line: check to see if your state opted to expand its Medicaid guidelines as per the new rules under the ACA. If they did, you might qualify for Medicaid.

4. Membership Organizations

Some organizations that cater to freelancers offer healthcare insurance. You can save a bundle by taking advantage of their group buying power. Two organizations to start with are Freelancers Medical (www.FreelancersMedical.org) and the National Association for the Self-Employed (www.nase.org).

It's also a good idea to check industry-specific organizations. For example, if you're a freelance writer, check out the healthcare plan offered by the National Writers Union (www.nwu.org).

Your local chamber of commerce may also be a good organization to investigate for health insurance. Many chapters offer a range of health-insurance products for their members.

5. Faith-Based (Christian) Health Plans

This is a growing phenomenon in the healthcare industry. Many faith-based healthcare programs are not insurance providers. However, they are set up as nonprofits that provide healthcare cost-sharing arrangements to those with the same religious beliefs. Because they are not insurance companies or providers, they are not licensed or regulated by any insurance board or department.

You must be a practicing Christian who lives according to biblical principles in order to qualify for a plan. This includes attending church regularly, foregoing tobacco and illegal drugs, and not abusing alcohol or legal drugs.

Some expenses that are generally excluded from coverage are routine checkups, preventive care, and dental and vision care. Costs tend to be lower than traditional market healthcare options as a result of these exclusions, by some estimates as much as 30 percent. Enrollees are encouraged to pay for these out of pocket to keep overall plan costs low for everyone.

Christian Healthcare Ministries (CHM), founded in 1982, was the first faith-based healthcare cost-sharing ministry. They can be found online at www.chministries.org.

6. Health Savings Account (HSA)

An HSA basically allows you to sock money away for a medical emergency tax-free. Health Savings Accounts were created in 2003 to give those with high-deductible health plans, as defined by the IRS, a tax-free way to save for medical expenses.

You can use money in an HSA account to pay for qualified medical expenses at any time with no federal tax liability or penalty.

To qualify for an HSA, you:

- Must be covered under a high-deductible health plan (HDHP)
- Can have no other health coverage except what is permitted under other health coverage as outlined in IRS guidelines
- Must not be enrolled in Medicare
- Can't be claimed as a dependent on someone else's 2015 tax return

So how much can you squirrel away each year in your HSA? For calendar year 2016, the annual limitation on deductions for an individual is $3,350. For family coverage, it's $6,750. You can contribute an additional $1,000 if you're fifty-five or older.

7. Spousal Insurance

This is one of the easiest routes to go if you're lucky enough to have this option. In most cases, you can just ask your spouse to add you to her plan.

The Best Healthcare Plan

There are more options than ever for freelancers to obtain healthcare coverage. The ever-raging battle though is cost. That's why it's important to investigate options. You may find, for example, that your spouse's corporate plan costs more than a faith-based option.

Healthcare—although totally tax deductible—is likely one of your most expensive overhead costs. Hence, it pays to investigate it every year as laws, rules, and enrollment periods are always changing. You definitely want to reassess your coverage when a major life event such as a marriage or having a baby happens.

The web makes it easy to compare all of these options via healthcare exchanges such as eHealthInsurance.com. They allow you to quickly and easily comparison shop for the best deals on healthcare plans for you and your family.

The ACA forever changed healthcare insurance in the United States. For the first time ever, coverage is available to everyone—even those with pre-existing conditions. You don't have to worry about not being able to get insurance just because you decide to go freelance.

And how freeing is that?

Chapter 14

Know Your Numbers

It's absolutely essential to your success as a freelancer that you know your numbers.

Many freelancers suffer from number-phobia, just like tons of other small business owners. When you're doing all the dreaming and planning and preparing for your new career, you may manage to gleefully sidestep the numbers.

Unless you're an accountant, who really wants to deal with numbers? This is why you're starting a freelance career anyway—to get away from the things that you don't like to do.

Unfortunately, not knowing your numbers will have you making a U-turn back to a nine to five so quick it'll make your head spin. If you don't know them, you'll be broke without knowing it; you'll be unable to pay your rent and not realize it until it's too late; you'll roll up to the ATM and stare in shock as the machine nastily spits out a receipt with a negative balance on it.

Six Numbers Freelancers Should Know

"Okay, okay," you're thinking. "You convinced me. I need to know my numbers. But which ones? What numbers are you talking about?"

1. Cash Flow

Various studies conducted over the last decade conclude that between 80 and 90 percent of small business failures can be attributed directly to cash flow problems. Cash flow is how much money is going out the door in relation to how much is coming in. It is a key report because it tells you two very important things about a freelancer's business, namely:

1. How a freelancer spends her money
2. How effective the freelancer is at collecting on invoices

This last point is particularly important because a freelance business can be profitable on paper, but still fail. If you aren't getting paid in a timely manner for jobs completed, then you won't have the "flow of cash" on hand you need to pay expenses.

Bills must be paid when they come due—whether or not you as a freelancer have collected on outstanding invoices. You can't call your landlord or utility company and say, "As soon as I get paid for that last job I completed, I'll send you a payment." The real world doesn't work in this manner. So even if you have enough in outstanding invoices to cover your expenses, if those invoices aren't paid in a timely manner, it can wreak havoc with your freelance business.

For example, let's say you have $10,000 in outstanding invoices, which are thirty days late. You have $7,000 worth of expenses that are due now, and only $5,000 in the bank. You're $2,000 short of the cash you need to pay your bills. How much would having that $10,000 in your account help?

Now imagine if this continues and the outstanding invoices start to pile up—and you have no idea when clients are going to pay. Yet, your monthly expenses remain the same; they're due the same time each month, whether you get paid or not. See how you can run into trouble?

This illustrates why cash flow is so important. Cash needs to flow into your freelance business on a regular basis so that you can meet your expenses as they come due—not when or if you're paid.

In order to stay on top of funds flowing in and out of your business, you should generate a cash flow statement at least once a month. FYI, following is what a simple cash flow statement looks like.

	JANUARY	FEBRUARY	MARCH	APRIL
STARTING CASH	1,000	1,200	900	(300)
IN				
Sales	1,000	1,100	1,200	1,200
Total In	2,000	2,300	2,100	900
OUT				
Payroll	300	500	600	400
Purchases	300	400	400	400
Overhead	200	500	400	300
Capital Expenses	0	0	1,000	0
Total Out	800	1,400	2,400	1,100
CASH BALANCE	1,200	900	(300)	(200)

How to Avoid Cash Flow Problems

To avoid running into cash flow problems:

- Have stringent payment and collection policies in place that include getting a certain percent upfront.
- Offer a small discount if an invoice is paid early.
- Don't let outstanding balances grow beyond a certain amount.
- Don't continue to work with clients who consistently pay late.

No matter how big the job is or how lucrative it is, if a client pays late, it puts your freelance business at risk. These are not good clients—no matter how much work they throw your way. Ethical businesses respect and adhere to payment deadlines. You can bet it's what they expect—and you should expect the same.

2. Gross Income

A freelancer's gross income consists of all monies earned before taxes and deductions. It is important because it is a key indicator of how well you're using (or not using) your resources to produce a profit.

For example, let's say you earn $40,000 one year as a freelance videographer. You run some numbers and realize that you could increase your earnings by at least 25 percent—and take on fewer clients—if you could do all your postproduction work in-house. So you spend $5,000 to buy the equipment you need to set up a postproduction studio in your home. The next year, you earn $55,200—a 38 percent increase in business; and you do so by having seven fewer clients than you did the previous year.

This is a good indicator that you're using your resources well to produce a profit. And the kicker is, you get more of a tax break because your postproduction studio is in a dedicated room in your home, which means you're entitled to all the tax breaks associated with a home office that are allowed by the IRS, as discussed later in this chapter.

3. Net Income

While knowing how much you earn (gross income) is great, the real truth of your earnings is this number. You haven't earned anything until you pay for it all—and this number tells you what you've earned after you've paid all business expenses.

If you earned $100,000 but your expenses were $100,001, then you lost money—only a dollar, but a loss is a loss—unless you build it into your business plan. Following are some circumstances under which you might take this course of action:

- You're just starting out and need to buy equipment
- Your business is growing and your home office is no longer sufficient, so you decide to rent a full-fledged office in a coworking space

- Personal reasons like expecting a child
- Going back to school to take a class to get certified for some discipline within your niche so you can charge more

As these examples illustrate, if you've built a loss into your business plan, you may still be on track to growing a successful freelance business. But if you haven't, then something's wrong and it's time to reassess.

4. Overhead/Expenses

These will be found on what's known as a profit and loss (P&L) statement. A P&L is simply a snapshot in time of what your business's sales and revenue (minus expenses) look like. P&Ls are usually generated quarterly, biannually, and/or annually.

Here is what a proper P&L statement looks like. See how expenses and revenues are categorized? Everything is accounted for and you can see it at a glance.

PROFIT AND LOSS STATEMENT FOR THE PERIOD ENDED:	
INCOME	**$**
Sales	00.00
Service	00.00
Other Income	00.00
Total Income	00.00
EXPENSES	**$**
Accounting	00.00
Advertising	00.00
Assets Small	00.00
Bank Charges	00.00
Cost of Goods Sold	00.00
Depreciation	00.00
Electricity	00.00

PROFIT AND LOSS STATEMENT FOR THE PERIOD ENDED:	
Hire of Equipment	00.00
Insurance	00.00
Interest	00.00
Motor Vehicle	00.00
Office Supplies	00.00
Postage and Printing	00.00
Rent	00.00
Repair and Maintenance	00.00
Stationary	00.00
Subscriptions	00.00
Telephone	00.00
Training/Seminars	00.00
Wages	00.00
Total Expenses	00.00
PROFIT/LOSS	**$000.00**

In the beginning, you're going to want to keep a close eye on your numbers, so you should generate a P&L statement at least quarterly. Because it lists all your business's income and expenses, it will give you great insight into how much you're spending where, and how to make realistic long- and short-term plans for the future.

5. Inventory

This applies only if you're in a product-based freelance business. Get used to thinking of inventory as "cash" instead of goods, because that's exactly what it is. It's cash masquerading as goods. Microsoft did a study that found the following:

To determine inventory productivity we use a measure called "turnover" which tells us how many times does inventory sell out in a year. In almost every segment of specialty retail—gift, clothing, sporting goods, jewelry, shoes, books, music, electronics, appliances, furniture, and many more—the stock turnover rates have held steady for over 25 years in the under 4 range and in a few cases, at less than 2 turns per year.

This means that for most of these stores they are carrying at least three months of sales in their store at any given moment, and in the case of books and some other categories, the inventory approaches a six-month supply at most times. . . .

Any inventory from four months to eight months old is considered slow moving and . . . inventory over eight months old is considered old inventory. . . .

You need to keep track of inventory excess because it costs you money—in storage, in reduced profits, in wasted capital. Remember, the shorter your sales cycle, the less inventory you can afford to keep on hand.

6. Customer Acquisition Cost (CAC)

This number goes directly to marketing. It tells you how much you can afford to spend to acquire a customer and still be profitable. If your freelance business's CAC is too high, you're going to run into trouble.

FREELANCER TIP

There are many free financial templates on the web to help you keep your finances straight.

If you don't want to invest in any bookkeeping or accounting software and your finances are relatively easy to keep track of, these can work just fine. Office.com, TidyForms.com, Google Docs, and WordsTemplates.org are four sites you can start with.

To compute it, calculate your entire cost of sales and marketing over a given period and divide it by the number of customers that you acquired during that period. Don't forget to include salaries and commissions for your employees in this formula.

This is why it's important to track your marketing efforts. You can drastically reduce your customer acquisition costs by cutting out ineffective marketing methods. However, if you don't know what they are, it's hard to know what to cut, which means you wind up not cutting anything for fear of cutting the wrong thing.

Three Things to Know about Taxes

One of the biggest mistakes many new freelancers make is carrying their full-time job tax-paying habits over into their freelance career. The rules are different for freelancing. Taxes take much more preparation when you freelance.

It can be exciting though because it will force you to get—and stay—intimate with your finances. This means you can become better prepared for major life happenings such as putting together a plan to get out of student loan debt, saving for a child's education, buying a home, and retirement. Following are three things every freelancer needs to know about taxes.

1. When to Pay

As a freelancer, your taxes will be due quarterly, not annually. As of this writing, you must make estimated tax payments quarterly if you expect to owe tax of $1,000 or more when you file your annual tax return. If you owe and you don't pay quarterly, you will be assessed penalties and interest by the IRS.

2. How Much to Set Aside

Another danger of waiting to pay at the end of the year is that you might not set aside enough money to cover your tax bill. If you're thinking, "But how do I know how much to pay? How do I estimate it?", the IRS has a form for that (of course they do). It's Form 1040-ES (Estimated Tax for Individuals).

A "quick and dirty" way to figure out your estimated quarterly taxes is to use a tax estimator calculator. For example, using Form 1040 for tax year 2015, if you were single and earned between $13,150 and $50,200, you would fall in the 15 percent tax bracket. So if your actual earnings were $40,000, you'd owe roughly $6,000 in taxes.

If that number astounds you, it should. Many freelancers are surprised at how much they owe compared to how little they earn. This is because you're paying taxes that your employer previously picked up, such as self-employment and Social Security taxes.

You pay based on net income, so your tax burden will be lower if your actual profit is lower. For this example, let's say your net earnings are $25,000. That's still a hefty $3,750 in taxes due. If you paid quarterly, it would only be $937.50 ($312.50 per month). That's an easier chunk to swallow than almost $4,000 at the end of the year—that you haven't saved for.

This is why it literally pays to get in the habit of setting aside an estimated percentage of earnings in a separate tax account to be paid quarterly. That's better than being caught with your tax bloomers down annually and having to pay fees and interest on top of a whopping amount that sends you into a full-blown panic.

3. Expenses You Can Legally Deduct

Freelancers fall into two groups when it comes to taking deductions. On the one hand, you have those who take every deduction, even those the IRS may later reverse, such as the home office deduction. On the other hand, you have those who just want to "get these things filed!" and take nowhere near the deductions they're legally entitled to. This costs because you could be leaving money on the table.

One of the beautiful things about freelancing is that you are entitled to a lot of deductions—and those deductions add up, even small ones you may not even think to include: subscriptions to industry publications, membership fees for networking events, and gas/mileage fees, and so on.

Be very clear about what deductions you can take and what you can't. The IRS outlines them all. If digging through this stuff is not the way you want to spend a lazy Sunday afternoon, hire a CPA. It will be money well spent—if for no other reason than you can be sure your taxes are done right.

The general lesson is you need to get really, really good at record-keeping when you start freelancing. Using productivity tools such as Evernote, you can easily scan receipts and records, turning them into easily categorizeable and storable files. This way, if you're ever audited by the IRS, you will be able to prove everything claimed on your return. Most panic at the thought of an IRS audit, but you don't need to. If you keep copious records, it's no cause for concern at all. It's just another business-related meeting you have to attend. That's the way to look at it. And hey, maybe after all is said and done they'll owe you a few bucks.

Retirement

Retirement is probably the event least planned for by freelancers. It's understandable because you're too busy trying to forge your own path and "live like no one else, so you can live like no one else," to borrow a phrase from get-out-of-debt guru Dave Ramsey.

But retirement is something you need to plan for. To this end, here's what every freelancer should know about retirement.

When to Start Saving for Retirement

Freelancers are responsible for their own retirement and it's something you have to be realistic about. Ideally, you should start saving for retirement from the day you open the doors of your new business. Realistically, many freelancers don't, especially during the first few years, but you need to make it a priority.

If you don't start putting aside money for retirement right out of the gate you are more likely to continue putting it off. So get in the habit of saving even if it is a nominal amount in the beginning. It will keep you aware that, "Hey, I have another responsibility over here that needs attention."

How to Save and How Much to Save

Financial planning experts suggest that freelancers save anywhere from 10 to 20 percent for retirement. Many find this a stretch, so if that's not possible, save the maximum you can contribute. As of this writing, the contribution limit for both traditional and Roth IRAs is $5,500, or $6,500 per year if you're fifty or older. Total annual contributions to both accounts—if you have both kinds—cannot exceed these limits. And yes you can have, and contribute to, a Roth IRA and a traditional IRA in the same year.

FREELANCER TIP

A Roth IRA is a special retirement account that self-employed individuals often choose because the money accumulates interest while in the account. You pay taxes on the money when you put it into the account, but all future withdrawals are tax-free. So overall, this system works very much in your favor.

Retirement planning can get very complicated because everyone has different goals and dreams. Hence, the best thing to do is consult a trusted financial advisor who can give you advice that's tailored to your life plan and your freelance business goals.

Retirement Account from a Previous Employer

If you have a retirement account with your previous employer, you have three options: cash it out, let it stay with your employer, or roll it over into an account of your choosing. Let's quickly assess each option.

Cash Out

Many freelancers use funds from their retirement account to start their business. If you're willing to take the IRS tax penalty hit of 30 percent, then go ahead (although I don't advise it). Twenty percent will be deducted by your employer for federal taxes, and if you're younger than fifty-nine-and-a-half years, another 10 percent will be deducted as an early withdrawal penalty.

FREELANCER TIP

In order to save more, you can look at any savings stashed in a Roth IRA account as a second emergency fund. See how creative you can be when saving for retirement as a freelancer? The point is, save something for retirement. Make it a habit from day one.

Keep It with Your Previous Employer

If you have a lot on your plate and don't want to deal with this aspect of your financial life right now, the easiest thing to do is to leave your account with your current employer. You can move your retirement account any time you want, so there's no immediate downside to leaving it. Note: many companies require a minimum of $5,000 be in the account.

Over the long haul, you do want to reassess this option because you'll essentially be out of the loop with what's happening at the company. If they, for example, change investment options, it could affect your account. So keep that in mind.

Do a Rollover

All this means is that you take the money in your current retirement account and roll it over into another retirement account, such as a Roth or other IRA account. It's like transferring funds between two bank accounts. As long as you don't take any disbursements, there are no IRS penalties or withdrawal fees.

If you choose this option, keep in mind that you can't just roll it over and forget it, as you most probably did with your account when you were employed full-time. You have to remember to add to it yourself because it will no longer automatically come out of your paycheck.

Consult a Financial Planner

Learning the basics of finances such as planning for retirement and how and when to pay taxes isn't difficult. It's just new, and hence it takes a little time to bone up on the specifics. But, if it's something that really rattles you or you don't want to do it, consider consulting a financial planner to get you on the right financial road for this new stage in your life.

FREELANCER TIP

A financial advisor is different from a certified financial planner. A financial advisor is anyone who gives you advice on finances—your accountant, your brother-in-law who's a stock broker . . . whoever. A financial planner is a certified finance expert who helps you to set realistic future goals by assessing your current situation and developing a realistic plan to help you meet them.

If tapping friends and family for referrals doesn't yield anyone you're satisfied with, visit www.NAPFA.org. It's the site for the National Association of Personal Financial Advisors.

Banking

As so much business is done on the web these days, it can be easy to slip into the habit of using your personal banking account for your freelance business. And why not? Especially if you decide not to incorporate, you can receive payments in your own name, and your name is already on your personal account. What's the big whoop about having a business account? That's just one more thing you're gonna have to manage.

Well, imagine this scenario.

April 15, 9:36 P.M. You wipe the sweat from your forehead, eyes flickering at the clock as the six changes to a seven. 9:37 P.M.

You have less than two and a half hours to go before you finish your taxes. You anxiously click over to the IRS site. What did they say about travel deductions again? Yes, you can take that deduction for those first three days in Seattle. Did you pay with your debit card or your credit card? What month was it again? Where is that receipt?

11:48 P.M. You've never been so glad to hit the "Send" button on a website in your life. Your taxes have been filed.

April 16, 12:32 A.M. With a glass of wine in hand, you look over the mass of paper on your desk and the number of windows open on your browser and vow never, ever to go through this nightmare again.

Filing your taxes has never been so convoluted, frustrating, and downright confusing. As you toss the paperwork on your desk into one big bag just to get it out of your sight, you realize that 75 percent of your angst could have been eliminated if you'd been more organized in your recordkeeping—and a big part of that is separating your business finances from your personal finances.

Three Financial Accounts Every Freelancer Needs

Following are the three financial accounts you need, at a minimum, as a freelance business owner.

1. Checking Account

This doesn't have to be a business checking account. It can be a personal checking account, but it should be used exclusively for your freelance business.

Personal accounts come with a lot of the foundational banking tools you need as a business: debit cards, overdraft protection, check cashing and handling, and direct deposits. The great thing about personal accounts is that they usually offer a certain number of free transactions before you get charged.

Business accounts offer the same conveniences as a personal checking account. Also, in many cases, you have access to a business banking manager who can offer advice on issues such as invoice factoring and small business loans. It's a great way to build a one-on-one relationship with a bank, especially if you foresee growing your business to the point where you need a line of credit or other bank services.

However, business accounts usually have fees such as monthly maintenance, transaction, and minimum balance fees that many personal accounts don't have, especially if you do all your banking online.

Compare the personal checking account option with the business checking account options offered by your bank. Note the fees. Then assess how you plan to bank. Asking the following questions will help you determine which type of checking account is right for your freelance business:

- Will I need the personal interaction of a teller, or will most of my transactions be done online?
- Will I require paper statements, or will I receive those electronically?
- How will I receive most of my payments—via check, credit card, or an online payment processor such as PayPal?
- Will the bulk of my payments be from domestic or international clients?
- How much do I plan to open the account with?
- What's the minimum monthly balance I know I can maintain?

Remember, in many cases, a personal checking account works just fine—especially the first few years. So don't just assume that because you're a business you need a business checking account. You don't. You could be spending an extra $20, $30, or $50 per month in unnecessary fees because your account is deemed "business" instead of "personal."

Comparison shopping for banks is as easy as shopping for shoes. Sites such as Bankrate (www.bankrate.com/checking), www.FindA BetterBank.com, and Credio (http://banks.credio.com) allow you to easily compare institutions on tangibles such as fees, interest rate, types of accounts offered, and more. They also allow you to shop locally by drilling down to a branch right in your zip code.

FREELANCER TIP

If you're sure you can do all your banking online, often going with a strictly online bank will save you money. So don't forget to keep this option in mind as you shop.

2. Online Payment Processor

In the age of the global economy, the world can be your customer base. Most expect to be able to pay via a trusted payment processor such as PayPal, discussed in Chapter 9.

Following are some other benefits of an online payment processing account:

- *Eliminate bank fees:* When you use a payment processor, the funds are placed in your account immediately. This eliminates the worry of bounced check fees. Also, you can eliminate some bank transaction fees, as much of the activity (payments, chargebacks) can take place in this account, then you can transfer funds to your bank account a few times per month as needed.

- *Legitimize your business:* When you register as a PayPal user, for example, you have to provide your name, address, phone number, and e-mail address. If you plan to purchase anything, you must also provide a credit card and/or bank account information. The fact that you are able to offer this option of payment legitimizes your business in the eyes of your customers.

• *Accept multiple payment options:* Payment processors allow buyers to pay by numerous methods, including eCheck, debit card, and credit card. So if a client doesn't have the cash on hand and wants to pay you via credit card, he can do so, which can drastically increase your income.

Payment processors such as PayPal, Authorize.Net, Google Wallet, and 2Checkout are safe, secure, trusted options for offering customers the option of paying online.

3. Credit Card

While you can use your personal credit card for business, of course, it will save you hours in paperwork come tax time if you get a credit card and use it strictly for business purposes.

Why put yourself through the hell every year of sorting purchases and expenditures from your personal accounts, sweating bullets come tax time, and swearing to do better next year. Get the credit card. File it away. Chunk business expenses on it. Easy, peezy! Following are a couple of other benefits of using a credit card:

1. Save money on fees: Usually, you can save money by paying for certain expenses on an annual instead of a monthly basis. Putting these on a credit card can be great if you don't have the cash on hand right away. Just be sure not to carry balances so long that you lose any savings because you're paying interest on a balance on your card. As soon as you're able, pay off the balance.

2. Rack up points and rewards: Almost all credit cards these days have some type of points and reward incentives that can be used for travel, gas, shopping, and so on. Even if you have the

cash on hand to pay, use these rewards and then pay off the balance of the card when the bill comes in.

This is the smart way to use credit cards. Try to never carry a balance on this card from month to month, and use it only for business purposes.

Financial Security

Once you set up these three accounts, set aside an administrative day or afternoon at least once a month to go through them, categorize the payments and expenditures, and log them into your bookkeeping or accounting records/software.

If you do this, come tax time you'll breeze through the filing process and can go on to more important things.

Chapter 15

Freelance Success Stories

Ever wonder how some freelancers manage to succeed while others fail? Following are success stories from six freelancers who share insight on freelance tangibles such as:

- How to get work from previous employers
- How to leverage "cheapie" gig sites such as Fiverr
- How to tell if your branding is working
- How and why they left their full-time jobs

No matter what type of freelance business you start, there's a nugget to be gleaned from each story.

From Inner-City Schoolteacher to Freelance Writer

Laura Pennington

I was an overworked and burned-out inner-city schoolteacher who had recently made the jump to corporate America when I realized that this wasn't going to fulfill me in the way that I had hoped it would. I stumbled across freelance writing while doing some Google searching during the summer of 2012, where I landed on www.Inkwell Editorial.com, among a few other sites.

Replacing My Full-Time Income

Within just a couple of months as a freelance writer I had met and surpassed my day-job income and realized that not only was I passionate about it but clients were giving me great feedback, indicating that I was a solid writer. Since then, I have expanded my freelance writing business to earn six figures a year and I left my day job.

How to Keep the Jobs Flowing In

In order to keep a continuous flow of work coming in, I focus specifically on clients who offer me monthly recurring work. This takes a lot of the challenge of chasing my own paycheck out of the equation because I know the clients are going to order a specific set of blogs every month, I know how to invoice them, and it's a lot easier to handle.

When you have clients with whom you work on an ongoing basis you also get to know their business extremely well and you can fine-tune your expertise in order to succeed as much as possible.

Why Saying "No" Can Be Profitable

Saying no to projects that are outside of my comfort zone has given me the time and flexibility to focus specifically on the projects that I do the best. I have a set financial income that I can expect every month just from my recurring clients, and I view anything on top of that as gravy.

It has also significantly lightened my marketing load. When I first got started as a freelance writer it was essential that I build my experience and get quality feedback and referrals from people. Now that I have a steady set of clients, some of whom I've been working with for two years or longer, I have to do much less marketing and can also be extremely choosy about whom I work with.

My Most Effective Marketing Method

My most effective marketing method has been to focus on a niche. When I first got started I would write for many different kinds of blogs and topics but I quickly realized that I had a great deal of expertise in the legal and insurance categories.

Focusing my business on those categories as well as my ideal clients within those subsections has allowed me to replicate my success over and over. I would pitch only to businesses that really fit into this niche because that was my comfort zone and I knew exactly what they needed and how to communicate with their clients.

At the beginning of your freelance writing career you might feel like you're throwing spaghetti against a wall and hoping that it will stick. Over time, though, you'll realize that you have the passion, the expertise, or both in order to succeed in a particular niche or a couple of niches.

My Number One Piece of Advice

Improve yourself. You need to educate yourself about SEO, about marketing, and you need to go into your freelance career every day acknowledging that you do not know everything. There is always something more that you can learn, and there are plenty of tools out there that are free or relatively inexpensive.

Be aware of your own weaknesses. This doesn't mean that a freelance writer needs to branch out and become a software developer but if you're writing in a particular niche, maybe you do some more reading about it or take an online course so that you understand the basics of the industry a little bit more.

Always being on top of your game also telegraphs to clients that you're extremely professional.

Good luck. You can do it—never doubt that!

Laura Pennington is a former teacher and marketing associate who found her passion with freelance writing. Since 2012, Laura has produced hundreds of unique content marketing pieces designed to help her legal and insurance clients build and grow their businesses. She now coaches freelancers on how to break through their income barriers with her program Six Figure Writing Secrets. She can be found online at www.SixFigureWritingSecrets.com and on Twitter @sixfigurewriter.

How to Turn a Past Employer Into a Freelance Client

Cathy Miller

Have you ever wished you acted on a dream sooner? My exit from a corporate career of thirty-plus years could be the poster child for staying too long at the party.

I had visions of freelancing years before. My inaction on that dream boiled over one day when I slammed down a phone during a call to a conference room full of senior executives. No, I did not get fired (thankfully, I had an understanding boss). However, I did quit my day job.

While I don't recommend such a dramatic exit, there are lessons to be learned on transitioning from a former employer to the life of a freelancer. Perhaps sharing a few tips will help you in your new freelancing career.

Tips for Gaining Freelance Work from Past Employers

After I dashed off my resignation letter, reality hit. I was no longer corporate employed. I needed clients. What better place to start than with people already familiar with my work? My former employers. The following tips may help you score freelancing gigs from a past employer.

Plan Your Exit

Perhaps you freelance on the side or have an exit date set in the future. Before you leave your current employer, plan your exit. Lay the groundwork for working with your soon-to-be-former employer.

Talk about making a smooth transition. Offer to continue unfinished projects or consult on others in your new capacity as an independent contractor.

Let your employer know you would love to have her as a client. Of course, this tip assumes that's true. If you'd rather cut off a hand than ever speak with your former employer, chances are you would not be a good match for future projects.

Share the benefits. No, not the health insurance kind (the loss of employer-sponsored benefits is one of the toughest pills to swallow). Discuss the benefits your employer gains by working with you as an independent contractor:

- It allows a smoother transition for work-in-progress
- Projects remain on track for meeting critical deadlines
- There is no learning curve—you already know their business
- They don't have to pay your employee benefits (a huge cost to an employer)

If you already left without having this discussion, initiate it now. Don't assume your former employer knows you want them as a client or can help them with unfinished projects. Most would welcome the extra help—especially after you point out the benefits.

Stay Current

Stay current on your former employer's business.

Use your inside knowledge. You have an incredible advantage over other freelancers—insider knowledge. You know how your former employer works. You know what projects have been stalled. You know what's been on their wish list. Use that knowledge.

Keep in touch. Connect through social media. Send your former employer an interesting article, report, or information useful to their business. Send holiday cards and if you had that kind of relationship, ask about their family or favorite charity. But keep it real and consistent. If you only get in touch asking for work, they will soon avoid your calls.

Follow their company. Congratulate them on new clients. Read about developments in their business or industry. The more you know, the easier it is to suggest specific projects. For example (if you are a freelance writer), "I saw the news about your new product's success. I think it would make a great case study story (or a featured article in *XYZ* magazine). I would love to share some ideas."

Suggest specific projects. Develop project ideas that benefit your former employer's current need and make the most of your freelance specialty.

Connect with the Past

Assuming you have more than one former employer, connect with others from your past. For me, the easiest path was through LinkedIn. You can choose the best vehicle for the type of work you do. The most lucrative is where your former employers do business.

Start with who you know. You may have stayed in touch with former employers or coworkers. Start there to see what's new, what's changed. Are the same people in charge? Who would be the best connection for your freelancing work?

Make your first contact a friendly experience. Think about the last time you ran into an old friend—one you had not seen in a long while. Wasn't it fun catching up? You found out what was going on in her life. She asked about yours.

Now think how you'd react if that person dominated the conversation with talk about her life and never once asked about yours. On top of it all, suppose she tries to sell you her company's latest product. Would you feel a bit put off? Most of us would.

LinkedIn made it easy for me to initiate a connection. The platform shares profiles of People You May Know. You can view their profiles and learn a lot about what's new. It's a perfect segue into reconnecting.

Hi, Mary. Your profile popped up on LinkedIn. It sure has been a long time since our days at ABC Company. I see you have a new position at GL Company. Congratulations! I would love to catch up.

Perhaps you use e-mail as an alternative. However you reconnect, think about that "it's all about me" person. Don't be that person.

Catch up. Be interested. You'll know when it's a good time to ask about possible work.

Follow your connection. You know one of the best things about employed people? They move around. I have had more than one connection leave a company and contact me to do work for them at their new company.

A bonus tip—broaden your connections within a company. Try to have more than one connection within a company. That way, when one connection leaves, you end up with work from both the first company and the new one.

Sweet.

Assuming you did not burn any bridges, former employers can be a great source for work. They trust your work and know you can deliver. Sometimes all it takes is reminding them of the benefits.

Cathy Miller is a freelance business writer with more than thirty years of professional experience. Cathy also specializes in healthcare, employee benefits, and wellness. Visit http://SimplyStatedBusiness .com for tips and free downloads to keep business communication simple, clear, and uniquely yours.

From Software Developer to Gaming Writer

Todd Mitchell

I never thought I could be a professional writer. I always wrote for fun, blogging and podcasting with friends about interests like video games, technology, and geek culture. One tweet—and the courage to jump at an opportunity—changed all that.

In the beginning of 2015, I was a senior software developer for a successful industrial engineering company and my wife was ending her term as a chief medicine resident at a prominent area hospital. We'd just moved into a house we'd purchased one month prior, and our first child was due within two weeks.

During my wife's time off with our newborn son, another hospital made my wife an incredible job offer, which initiated serious discussions about our family's future. We became interested in caring for our son ourselves. My wife couldn't work from home, but we realized I could leave my job, care for the baby, and support the family by working on software independently. At age twenty-nine, I put in my notice and retired from a career more than a decade in the making.

One Fateful Tweet

I pursued game development, a lifelong dream, with everything I had. I cared for our son during the day and worked after bedtime on projects I felt deeply about. I worked hard, but newborn care made project management nearly impossible. I frequently used Twitter to network and draw inspiration from colleagues. That's how I saw the tweet.

"RT: We're expanding our editorial focus and we're looking for new freelancers!"

This editor worked for a large network of gaming sites. They did what my friends and I did with blogging, but for money. Maybe it was the transitional time I was in or the numbness I felt from recent failures, but I reached out without hesitation.

In an e-mail that was probably too long, I introduced myself and explained why I might make a good contributor for their site. The editor kindly e-mailed back, letting me know I would need to submit writing samples or a portfolio to be considered. This oversight was embarrassing.

I was discouraged; she advertised top rates for writers and would surely attract the best in the industry. Still, I scraped together every coherent blog post, article, and casual game review I'd written recently, even harvesting posts from an old WordPress XML backup, and sent over the best content I could before resolving to forget the whole thing. At least I had a new idea for potential income.

Scrambling to Learn How to Freelance

An unexpected response came later that evening.

"I'll definitely read pitches from you!" The editor laid out the freelancer terms and rates, all of which were pleasantly surprising. I thanked her and promised I would be sending pitches very soon. I was a real freelancer with no idea what I was doing.

I scrambled to learn how freelance journalism works, scoured old grammar books, and racked my brain for article ideas. I pitched ideas the following week and sold my first feature proposal for over $1,000. Since that time I've sold articles, expanded my professional network, started blogging routinely, and I hope to finish my first book in 2016.

The Number One Piece of Advice I'd Give

Aspiring freelancers have to be prepared to strike when opportunity arises. Be ready to push fear and doubt aside and put your best work in front of someone who scares you.

If you're writing online, perform ongoing portfolio maintenance (I love www.Contently.com for this) so you're ready at a moment's notice. Constantly expand your platform: blog, submit paid work and guest posts far and wide, and participate (not just promote) on social media.

Develop a talent for *finding* opportunity. Know who the decision-makers are. In my case, just searching Twitter for "game editor" showed me the editors for *Game Informer*, Ars Technica, the *Guardian*, Yahoo! Games, MTV, IGN, and countless others. There's no excuse for wondering where to turn for opportunities.

Learn from the greats. Nathan Meunier, a well-known industry freelancer, has written incredible answers to nearly every question I had while getting started. Every field has an expert; find yours.

Finally, never let up. You provide content or a service that is desperately needed. Your level of success will be determined by your ability to find that need.

Todd Mitchell is a game industry journalist with experience in professional software and indie game development. Follow him on Twitter @mechatodzilla, and visit him online at http://Code WritePlay.com.

How to Master Branding

Jennifer Brown Banks

Major players in the business to consumer arena can measure the effectiveness of their branding efforts through revenue, market share, and the supply and demand associated with their particular product. The proof is in the pudding. In a sea of many, they dominate the market and emerge as what is commonly known as "household names."

But how do you know if your expensive website, guest posts, products, social media shares, and other marketing activities have successfully established your brand, "sold" others on the value of what you have to offer, and distinguished you from the vast competition?

Not knowing means that you could be wasting time, money, and resources with little or no return on your investment. It also translates into a platform that will more than likely lack a solid foundation. Of course, you could consult your site's analytics and hope for clues, or continue to take shots in the dark. But, there's a better way.

Before I reveal the specifics, let's look at the "big picture" of what successful branding entails, and why it's imperative to get it right.

According to the book *Shark Tank Jump Start Your Business*, based off the popular reality show, "A brand is much bigger than just a product or service. It's the emotional response to your business—the visual and psychological representation of your identity."

It further states, "Many small business owners are under the impression that branding is reserved for larger companies with millions or billions of dollars. But nothing could be further from the truth."

With this in mind, from a strategic standpoint, here's what your branding should take into consideration.

VISUAL FACTORS
- Your logo
- Your website/blog design
- Your slogan

- The colors of your website
- Business cards
- The quality of your website content

NONVISUAL FACTORS

- Your voice: Your personality, style of expression, and tone.
- Your online reputation with those in your niche community: Keep in mind that being "well known" and "well regarded" are two different things. For example, James Frey, Charlie Sheen, and Monica Lewinsky are all well known. Get the idea here?
- Your interaction with industry professionals: There's great truth to the expression, "We are judged by the company we keep." The more you are able to be in the same top-rated places where others in your niche congregate, the greater the perceived value of your brand.
- Awards received: Industry recognition goes a long way in strengthening your brand, boosting your image, and increasing your bottom line. Case in point: The first advertiser I ever got at my site surfaced immediately after I placed as a finalist in *Write to Done*'s annual Top 10 Contest. A publisher in Arizona initiated contact with me to discuss promoting her product.
- Psychological effect: Think of it like word association. What do people idenify your brand with? Prosperity? Excellence? Success? Innovation?
- Your credibility and expertise: This might include authoring a bestselling or popular book in your niche.
- Longevity in your niche community: The longer the better.

Three Ways to Tell If Your Branding Is Working

Aside from the elements listed previously, here's how to assess whether your branding efforts are building your business:

1. You spend less time on marketing and cultivating new business than when you started out. Clients routinely come to you

without direct pitches on your part—due to your expertise, reputation, or referrals. Here's an e-mail from a recent client as an example: "I've enjoyed your blog since following your comment from Think Traffic and think you're one of the best on the topic of writing for the web. I've been struggling a bit on my blog's reboot. Do you consult for a fee?"

2. You're considered a thought leader and influencer among your peers. Others in your niche seek your perspective on important issues. They want to pick your brain and get your "two cents" via interviews, reviews, and round-up articles.

3. You garner investor confidence. Advertisers are spending money with you with the belief that your "brand" is worth affiliating with their brand. For example, if your site accepts ads, are ad spots filled? This speaks volumes about your perceived success, and your ability to stand out (and deliver) in your niche area.

Remember that the more your brand works, the less you have to.

Use these guidelines to "work smarter, not harder," and take the guesswork out of building your brand and your bottom line.

Jennifer Brown Banks is a veteran freelance writer, content creator, award-winning blogger, and relationship columnist. Her work has appeared extensively online and in print publications including: *ProBlogger, Write to Done, Men with Pens, Tiny Buddha*, and *Chicago Sun-Times*. When she's not busy at the keyboard, she loves being "creative" in the kitchen. Visit her site *Pen & Prosper* (www.PenandProsper.blogspot.com), which was rated one of the Top 100 Blogs for Writers.

Leverage "Cheap Gig Sites" to Earn a Full-Time Living

Top-Rated Fiverr Seller Akira007

I've been a top-rated seller on Fiverr for three years. I offer a few services, mainly CreateSpace book covers and all kinds of Photoshop services. I know many don't hold sites like Fiverr in high regard, but I've managed to make a full-time living doing what I'm good at.

Make Money Quick

When I first got started on Fiverr, there weren't as many sellers as there are now. As the site has grown, many have discovered it, and newbies quickly think, "It's a good way to make some fast cash."

These are usually starry-eyed newbies who are mostly looking at top-rated sellers with 100k-plus gigs sold and think, "He must be a millionaire." Um, not so much.

There are very successful "giggers" on Fiverr who have managed to earn big bucks and do things like buy a house, make a living traveling the world, and transition from full-time jobs, but what all of them have in common is that they work hard. Many of them have built their businesses to the point where they have people working for them. Hence, they're not solo sellers.

So don't start with a "make money quick" mentality. You're building a business—give it the in-depth time, thought, and preparation it deserves, just like any other business.

The Attraction of Fiverr

The attraction of Fiverr is the low price. When you log on, think, "What am I willing to do for $5 that I can build on and turn into higher-paying gigs?"

Think logically. In the beginning, it's probably only going to be you, slogging away at $5 per gig. So be sure to choose a service that allows you to produce quickly enough so you can make a decent living.

When I first started out, there were no gig "packages" like there are now, where you can immediately start to earn more than $5 for a product/service, so I did some research to see how I could gain repeat customers. To get firsthand info, I became a site user instead of just a Fiverr seller. While a lot of the work I ordered was good, a lot of it was bad too.

I was astounded at just how low some of the quality was. I immediately saw my opening. I knew I could do better. So, I did, going over and beyond on each order. This got me recognized by the Fiverr staff, who awarded me a top-rated seller star, which took my business to another level.

So that's my story.

Seventeen Steps to Selling Success

Following is what I call my "seller's bible." They are the steps I took to leverage the popularity of the site to build a mobile business that earns me a full-time living. I'm not special or unique. What I am is a firm believer that anyone can do the same if they really want to.

1. Decide What to Sell

I looked at all the gigs being offered within the skill set I had and settled on eBook covers because a lot of sellers were offering this service, so I knew it had to be popular; and I found a group that was being underserved in this niche—eBook covers for CreateSpace. No one was targeting this niche at the time.

2. Assess the Competition

Ask yourself, "What can I do better?" What USP (unique selling point) can I build my gig around? What will make me stand out from the competition? What can I offer that they're not?

3. Make an Eye-Catching Gig Page

Your gig page should "pop" and be professional. Nothing amateurish. There are a lot of quality businesses who offer their services on Fiverr. You're competing against them. So don't think that just because the site is advertised as "Get anything for $5" that you can throw anything up and get work. You won't. Don't forget this.

4. Price Your Gig Right

Remember, you can offer gig packages, which means you can start off right out of the gate earning more than $5.

To get customers, you might be tempted to price cheaply when you first start. But why compete on price, especially when it's already so low. Trust me, if someone doesn't want to pay even $5 for a service, getting it from you for cheaper will not attract the types of clients you want to cultivate.

Why not charge more if you're confident that the service you offer is a good one for which you know people will pay more (and you are offering a legitimate, professional service, right?).

In my experience, the cheaper you go, the worse you'll be treated; buyers will want constant revisions, demand unreasonable turna-round times, and so on. If you don't deliver, they'll give you a low rating, which decreases your odds of landing other gigs.

It's not worth it. Price your work higher. It may take longer to land clients, but it'll be worth it in the end because you'll be building a client base that's not into competing on the lowest price.

5. Focus on Quality

Nice work, or fast work?

Umpteen people offer "get it quick" gigs. You'll promptly get lost in that shuffle, and more than likely, your quality will suffer.

Again, if you're offering an in-demand service like videos and graphic design along with stellar quality, why should you sell yourself "fast and cheap?"

Exception: If you have a push-button gig that doesn't require a huge time expenditure (i.e., the software does the work for you), then this can be the way to go. But more often than not, offering a fast gig is a bad idea.

6. Use Front-Page Positioning

When you present a new gig, it will be on the front page of Fiverr for the first fourteen days. Use this time wisely to promote, promote, promote your gig—on social media, on your website, on free classified ad sites.

After those fourteen days, your gig will go to sleep for a while, which means no one will see it unless they're searching by specific categories and your gig pops up, or if you're a "featured."

7. Be Patient

If you last three months on Fiverr, you should start getting regular customers if you've done good work, and especially if you've gotten great feedback.

8. Target Return Customers

You definitely want return customers. Doesn't every business? They're your meat and potatoes—and gravy and biscuits!

My gig was set up from the beginning to attract repeat customers who will always return because I did great work and provided excellent customer service. This means they more than likely left excellent feedback; a five-star rating is always the goal. The overwhelming majority will have no problem providing that if they're happy with your work.

This is another reason to really think about your pricing in the beginning. Competition on price on a site where rates are already rock-bottom is a recipe for disaster. A low rating is deadly for a gigger, especially in the beginning, and those who are looking for the cheapest work are almost always the ones who will leave this type of feedback if they're not happy about even the smallest thing.

9. Handling "Buyers from Hell"

These are the types of customers who will let you work and work and work, asking for change after change after change—and even when you've done your best to comply, they still leave you bad feedback.

This is exactly what you don't need, especially in the beginning. So how do you avoid this?

Assess how the customer is acting when you deliver his first order. If you know you did a good job and he immediately presses the modification button, telling you to change everything, red flag, red flag, red flag.

You're going to be upset, maybe even a little angry. So the first thing you want to do is calm down.

If a client makes what you consider an unreasonable request on a job you know you've done your best on and suspect he'll never be happy, just tell him that you don't understand the changes and/or cannot complete them. Then immediately offer a full refund.

Why a full refund, especially as you've done work you know he most likely intends to use anyway? Your goal is to get him to go away without leaving negative feedback. By the way, this happens very rarely—in maybe 1 out of 100 customers. So don't stress.

After you offer a full refund to your customer, write customer service on Fiverr. Apprise them of the situation. Let them know you want to give the customer a full refund. They'll honor that request and remove any negative feedback a customer might have left.

Always deliver your work with a watermark until the customer is happy. This way, you will never lose your work, because he can't use watermarked material anywhere else (unless he pays someone to remove the watermark).

10. Stay in Contact with the Fiverr Team

E-mail them. When in doubt ask questions about anything: their policies, how to handle a sticky situation with a customer, how to improve your rating, etc. This puts you on their radar as someone who's interested in providing the best service possible on the site. And it just might garner you the coveted Top-Rated Seller badge.

FYI, no one knows how Fiverr selects its top-rated sellers, so getting a reputation as trying to provide a good service can only help.

11. Check in Regularly

Always check your mailbox and answer buyers as quickly as possible. Usually, buyers are contacting multiple sellers, so the faster you answer, the more you increase your chance of getting the gig.

12. Communicate, Communicate, Communicate

Communicating well with your clients completes half the job. Understanding what they want before you start will cut down on possible revisions and requests for changes. The more detail, the better, so don't be afraid to ask lots of questions. Also, it shows customers right from the start that you want to do the best job possible, which goes a long way in building a great relationship.

13. Be Realistic about Deadlines

Don't work yourself to death; be realistic when you set deadlines. If you have twenty gigs running, what will happen when you have 100 orders?

Always set your delivery time to what's possible for you. Yeah, many customers want one-day gigs, and that's what you want to offer, but will you be able to deliver more than three, four, or five of them in a timely manner? As you get busier, you can think about bringing on help—if you've priced your gig right and can afford to pay for it.

14. Mentally Prepare to Work Hard

Fiverr is no gift shop that hands out dollar bills. Maybe that was the case five years ago, but today, it's more like Wall Street. It will eat you, say thank you for the money you made for us, spit you out, and bring in another crop of fifty doing the same thing tomorrow.

The way to beat this? Target repeat clients. Price your services well. Provide excellent customer service. Excel at quality. All the things I've listed thus far.

15. Remember That the Customer Is King

Always try to deliver a good product. Sometimes people have strange tastes and you may think what they want is crap and you can make it better. However, if they insist that *x* is what they want, then give it to them.

Fluorescent orange could have been their dead grandmother's favorite color, even though it makes their eBook cover look cheap and garish. You never know what their motivation is and it isn't your business to know. Your job is to make them happy by giving them what they want, provided it's within your skill set. As long as you achieve this goal, then keep it moving.

16. Don't Be Afraid to Say No

Always listen carefully to what your customer wants, and if it's something you can't provide, don't be afraid to turn the gig down. A simple, "I'm sorry, I'm unable to complete this order. Thank you for considering me, though. I really appreciate it. Good luck finding someone."

Rather than risk getting into a lengthy job that the customer may not be happy with (and she winds up giving you bad feedback), just say no from the beginning. It'll save you a lot of headaches.

17. Limit the Number of Gigs

I recommend listing no more than ten gigs in the beginning. I started with three, which is what I still have (see how doing all that research about what to offer in the beginning can pay off).

These keep me plenty busy because I have the all-important "returning customer." Over 150 of those I've done work for come back and place orders with me month after month, and that's more than enough for me to earn a great living.

I'm on Fiverr at www.Fiverr.com/users/akira007 if anyone has further questions, or wants additional insight.

What Freelancing Taught Me about Money, Self-Worth, and Honing My Craft

Anne Wayman

I've learned three major lessons along my way to a successful writing career. The first was learning how to boost my own self-worth. The second was learning how to handle money. For me both issues were linked. The third lesson is writing also takes practice.

Boosting My Self-Worth

I had somehow grown up believing almost anyone could write well. That meant, of course, that my writing wasn't very valuable. I first began to suspect I had an above-average skill when I worked for a magazine. Every month I completed my assignments long before anyone else. The editor there was kind enough to confirm my observation. I was so glad that I dared ask!

Later, when I began editing publications myself, I was appalled at what even pro writers sent in, expecting and getting total rewrites. There really is a lot of dreck in the world.

Little by little I realized that most people can't write well and my skill, which has only gotten better over time, is indeed valuable. I remind myself of that often—and particularly any time I need a self-worth boost.

Ultimately I also realized that how I view myself is really my choice. I've deliberately worked at noticing what I do well and how much I get done. It makes much more sense to focus on my talents than to spend a lot of time bemoaning the fact I rarely make my bed.

The lesson for new freelancers: recognize your talent. Don't shy away from it or undervalue it, especially if it's going to be your career. After all, if you don't believe in your talent, how can you get others to see the value in it—and pay you for it!

Learning to Handle Money

There was a time in my life when I'd creep up to the ATM hoping that I'd have money in my accounts. Some good friends gradually helped me understand that being conscious of my money was the only thing that made sense.

First I learned to track every single penny. These days I use a program called You Need a Budget, or YNAB (www.ynab.com), because it's simpler than the better-known bookkeeping programs and they don't charge for updates. Besides, I like their philosophies about money. I can relax a bit and if I'm off in one of my accounts, I can just make an adjustment.

What surprised me was how much getting control of my income and expenses by tracking my money not only helped my bottom line but increased my self-worth as well. Today, I can have discussions with clients, friends, family, and even bankers about my money not only without fear, but with real confidence. That's a real blessing.

The lesson for new freelancers: don't shy away from money—that includes everything from how you set your rates to what you sock away for retirement. You are a for-profit business; you're not a charity who's just grateful to get a client. I've learned that money, for most, is inextricably linked to self-worth—not that you value it for the sake of valuing it, but rather as one measure of your talent, the worth you bring to clients, and how you view yourself in relation to your competition. If you don't value your talent, who will?

I Practice My Art

I'm a writer and I write most days. I've been writing long enough so that if I miss a day or two, I don't panic. I trust my writing, my ability to write, and my ability to write well. If I get stuck, I either keep writing until I have a breakthrough or switch to another project.

The lesson for new freelancers: someone once said—maybe it was even me—that "it's hard to get worse at something you practice." I've found that to be true with my art, my writing, and even my money.

Even when you don't have a paid project on your desk, there's always something you can be doing to get better at your craft—whatever it is.

Although we're all unique, I know that we are all also the same. That's one of life's paradoxes. My hunch is any artist at any age can benefit from these three lessons, and the earlier the better.

As always, write well and often.

Anne Wayman has been successfully writing as a freelancer for longer than she cares to admit. You can find her writing blog at www.AboutFreelanceWriting.com and her professional site at www.AnneWayman.com. She also ghostwrites books and coaches writers.

Why So Many Freelance Writers?

By now, you may be thinking, "There are a lot of freelance writers featured. I wonder why?"

The short answer is, because of the growth of the web, it's a much-needed skill that a lot of businesses are investing in. Let me expand on that a bit.

The Changing Face of the Worldwide Workforce

In 2012, Upwork (then Elance) conducted a global business survey comprised of 1,500 businesses from around the world who hired freelance talent. Following are some of the key findings reported by survey respondents:

- Online freelance talent was better than or equal to what was available to them locally.
- More than half (54 percent) said that their workforce would be online in five years.
- Eighty-five percent reported that hiring online talent gave them an advantage over competitors.
- Cost savings averaged 53 percent.

The Five Most Sought-After Skills in Online Freelance Professionals

There are many types of online businesses aspiring freelancers can start. Following are five of the most common, which cost little or nothing to start, are mobile in that they can be done from anywhere there's an Internet connection, and are in strong demand due to the digital, global economy. The percentage numbers represent the number of people working in each field as freelancers.

1. Web programming/development (70 percent)
2. Graphic design/multimedia experts (61 percent)
3. Writing/content creation/blogging (38 percent)
4. Online marketing/social media consulting (32 percent)
5. Mobile development (28 percent)

Conclusion

In the last decade, Americans have weathered a crippling mortgage/foreclosure crisis, they have witnessed big banks and other corporations fail at alarming rates, and they have seen the economy tank to levels not seen since the Great Depression—and as a result have been laid off, fired from "stable" jobs, and seen their pensions and retirement savings shrink to practically nothing. Many have taken retirement off the table altogether, working longer and harder just to keep food on the table and a roof over their heads. They are tired—tired of . . .

- The uncertainty
- Not being able to make a living wage
- Not being in control of their own financial destiny
- Wall Street getting bailed out while they are left out in the cold

Who's been around to witness all of this? Millennials. And they're asking, "Is there a better way?"

With the aggressive invention and mainstream use of mobile technology like Skype, tablets, smartphones, and file sharing, the last decade or so has created a perfect storm of conditions for freelancing to thrive—and it has. In fact, you could argue that freelancing *is* the new job stability.

Bibliography

Allen, David. *Getting Things Done: The Art of Stress-Free Productivity.* (London: Penguin Books, 2015.)

Birkinshaw, Julian and Jordan Cohen. "Make Time for the Work That Matters." *Harvard Business Review,* September 2013. https://hbr.org/2013/09/make-time-for-the-work-that-matters.

Blakeman, Chuck. "Richard Branson Is Right: Time Is the New Money." Inc.com, September 30, 2014. www.inc.com/chuck-blakeman/richard-branson-is-right-time-is-the-new-money.html.

Bloom, Steve. "Time Is the Most Important Thing You Own." http://dosomethingcool.net/time-important.

Branch, Allen. "Getting Sued." Creative Class. https://creativeclass.io/getting-sued.

Brighton Fuse. "Brighton Fuse 2: Freelancers in the Creative Digital IT Economy." January 2015. www.brightonfuse.com/wp-content/uploads/2015/01/brighton_fuse2_online.pdf.

Clear, James. "The Only Productivity Tip You'll Ever Need." http:// jamesclear.com/productivity-tip.

comScore. "2015 U.S. Digital Future in Focus." www.comscore .com/Insights/Presentations-and-Whitepapers/2015/2015-US-Digital-Future-in-Focus.

Content Marketing Institute. "Advancing the Practice of Content Marketing." http://contentmarketinginstitute.com.

Cowork|rs. "The Complete Guide to Coworking in NYC." www .alleywatch.com/2014/01/the-complete-guide-to-coworking-in-nyc.

Duggan, Maeve. "The Demographics of Social Media Users." Pew Research Center, August 19, 2015. www.pewinternet.org/2015/ 08/19/the-demographics-of-social-media-users.

Ferriss, Tim. "The Best Tools and Apps to Boost Your Productivity in 2016." Inc.com, January 14, 2016. www.inc.com/tim-ferriss/the-best-tools-and-apps-to-boost-your-productivity-in-2016.html.

Gillum, Scott. "The Disappearing Sales Process." ForbesBrand*Voice*, January 7, 2013. www.forbes.com/sites/gyro/2013/01/07/ the-disappearing-sales-process.

Gray, Bev. "Wanna Be a Writer?" January 25, 2016. www.linkedin .com/pulse/wanna-writer-bev-gray.

Hera Hub. "Why Coworking?" http://herahub.com/about/ why-coworking.

ISPO News. "90 Percent of All Purchasing Decisions Are Made Subconsciously." http://mag.ispo.com/2015/01/90-percent-of-all-purchasing-decisions-are-made-subconsciously.

Jansen, Liza. "The Best (and Cheapest) Places in the World for Coworking." *Quartz*, March 31, 2015. http://qz.com/371714/ the-best-and-cheapest-places-in-the-world-for-coworking.

Keohane, Dennis. "Elance-oDesk Rebrands As Upwork, Starts New Chapter As the Freelance Marketplace for the Information Age." PandoMedia, May 5, 2015. https://pando.com/2015/05/05/elance-odesk-rebrands-as-upwork-starts-new-chapter-to-connect-workers-with-businesses-faster.

Kruse, Toke. "3 Reasons Why Some Freelancers Get More Jobs Than Others." Elance, April 9, 2013. www.elance.com/q/ blog/3-reasons-why-some-freelancers-get-more-jobs-others.

Margulies, Danny. "How I Built a 6-Figure Freelancing Business on Elance." Millo.co. http://millo.co/ how-i-built-a-6-figure-freelancing-business-on-elance.

Paul, Marla. "Natural Light in the Office Boosts Health." Northwestern University, August 8, 2014. www.northwestern.edu/ newscenter/stories/2014/08/natural-light-in-the-office-boosts-health .html.

Popova, Maria. "The Psychology of Self-Control." *Brain Pickings*. www.brainpickings.org/2013/11/27/the-psychology-of-self-control.

Rider, Elizabeth. "The Reason Vision Boards Work and How to Make One." *Huffington Post*, January 12, 2015. www.huffington post.com/elizabeth-rider/the-scientific-reason-why_b_6392274.html.

Shapiro, Ed and Deb. "Why Saying 'No' Is Saying 'Yes' to Yourself." *Huffington Post*, August 10, 2010. www.huffingtonpost.com/ed-and-deb-shapiro/why-saying-no-is-saying-y_b_674795.html.

Smith, Anthony. "3 Ways to Scale Your Business When You Don't Have a Ton of Resources." *Fortune*, January 16, 2016. http://fortune .com/2016/01/16/scale-startup.

Taussig, Alex. "How to Know If Your Business Will Scale." *Fortune*, June 1, 2011. http://fortune.com/2011/06/01/ how-to-know-if-your-business-will-scale.

"The Top 10 Web Hosting Companies of 2016." www.top10best websitehosting.com/international-comparison.

Vista Health Solutions. "Health Insurance Hardship Exemptions from the Affordable Care Act." NYHealthInsurer.com, May 19, 2014. www.nyhealthinsurer.com/2014/blog/health-insurance-hardship-exemptions-from-the-affordable-care-act/.

Wagner, Eric T. "My Journey: From Pan-Handler to Seven Figures." Mighty Wise Academy. http://mightywisemedia.com/my-journey.

—"5 Steps to Scale Your Business (You Won't Make It Otherwise)." *Forbes*, November 20, 2013. www.forbes.com/sites/ericwagner/ 2013/11/20/5-steps-to-scale-your-business-you-wont-make-it-otherwise/#ccfe5ce29e45.

Index